TELESCOPE POWER

Fantastic Activities & Easy Projects for Young Astronomers

GREGORY L. MATLOFF

with drawings by Constance Bangs

A Professor Wiley Book

John Wiley & Sons, Inc.

New York • Chichester • Brisbane • Toronto • Singapore

In recognition of the importance of preserving what has been written, it is a policy of John Wiley & Sons, Inc., to have books of enduring value published in the United States printed on acid-free paper, and we exert our best efforts to that end.

Library of Congress Cataloging-in-Publication Data
Matloff, Gregory L.
    Telescope power : fantastic activities and easy projects for young
astronomers / Greg Matloff.
        p.   cm.
    Summary: An introduction to the telescope and its uses, including
information on setting up the equipment, observation techniques, and
a variety of projects and experiments.
    Includes index.
    ISBN 0-471-58039-2 (pbk.)
    1. Telescopes—Experiments—Juvenile literature.   2. Astronomy—
Experiments—Juvenile literature. [1. Telescopes—Experiments.
2. Astronomy—Experiments. 3. Experiments.] I. Title.
QB88.M378   1993
522'.2'078—dc20   92-39602

Printed in the United States of America
10 9

Contents

5 ★ *Tracking the Planets*   66

6 ★ *Following the Stars*   82

7 ★ Observing the Sun   100

When I heard the learned astronomer,
When the proofs, the figures, were ranged in columns before me,
When I was shown the charts and diagrams, to add, divide,
    and measure them,
When I sitting heard the astronomer where he lectured with
    much applause in the lecture room,
How soon unaccountable I became tired and sick,
Till rising and gliding out I wandered off by myself,
In the mystical moist night air, and from time to time,
Looked up in perfect silence at the stars.

—Walt Whitman, "When I Heard the Learn'd Astronomer" (1865),
from *Leaves of Grass*

Introduction:
What's Up There?

Congratulations! Now you own a telescope or have decided to buy one. You're eager to assemble the gleaming components of the new instrument and point it toward the sky. But before you begin to observe the heavens, let's consider what's up there, in the vast spaces above the confines of the Earth's atmosphere. Our explorations will start at the top of our planet's 200-kilometer (120-mile) ocean of air and continue to the most distant sky objects that can be observed with a small telescope—stars so far away that the light seen from them has been traveling for millions of years.

You'll start by viewing mountains and craters on the Moon. Soon, you'll keep track of the phases of the neighboring planet Venus and seasonal changes on Mars, that beckoning world that may someday become a second home for humanity. Moving farther into space, you'll learn about the large satellites of Jupiter (the largest of the worlds that circle our Sun) and the beautiful rings of the second largest planet in our solar system, Saturn. Colorful stars—some single like the Sun and others grouped with companions—will become your landmarks in the night sky.

A Sister to the Earth

To the unassisted (or naked) eye, the Moon looks like a big marble hanging in the sky. Through binoculars or a low-power telescope, our planet's one natural satellite is revealed as a world in its own right. Clearly visible are the vast, relatively flat plains (called *maria*) where the Apollo astronauts landed, mountains that rival the tallest on Earth, and craters resulting from cosmic impacts billions of years in the past.

Children of the Sun

Earth and eight other worlds (Mercury, Venus, Mars, Jupiter, Saturn, Uranus, Neptune, and Pluto) circle the Sun in closed paths called *orbits*. Like our Moon and other satellites, the planets shine by reflected sunlight.

Mercury, the closest world to the Sun, is often lost in the Sun's glare and is difficult to view from most locations. Very far from the Sun and Earth are Uranus, Neptune, and Pluto. Although these planets were discovered with the aid of the telescope, most amateur astronomers concentrate their planetary attention on Venus, Mars, Jupiter, and Saturn.

Through your telescope, Venus shows a yellow-white disk that changes with the planet's phases. Nothing can live within the dense, hot cloud cover of this neighboring world.

Mars shows seasonal changes. With moderate magnification and a good viewing location, you can view this red planet's white polar caps, as they grow in Martian winter or shrink during the Martian summer.

The giant planet Jupiter puts on an incredible sky show. This world has colorful cloud bands that can be easily observed through a small telescope. Within Jupiter's cloud bands you can view the Great Red Spot—a turbulent zone large enough to gobble up the Earth with room to spare! The largest of Jupiter's many satellites—Callisto, Europa, Ganymede, and Io—can be observed through low-power binoculars, even though Jupiter never ventures closer to Earth than about 600 million kilometers (400 million miles).

The next planet out, Saturn, is the last of the planets that we can find with the naked eye. Smaller than Jupiter (although still much larger than Earth), this giant world is considered by many to be the most beautiful object in the sky. Although all of the giant worlds are encircled by rings, only Saturn's rings are bright enough to be visible in a small telescope.

Visitors in the Skies

There are a number of smaller members of the solar system that can be observed in the night sky. The closest of these are our planet's artificial satellites. As you become familiar with the natural objects in the heavens, you'll sometimes notice the reflected sunlight from large artificial Earth satellites, as these spacecraft move across the evening sky.

The naked-eye observer will sometimes witness the track of a meteor, or "shooting star," as this piece of celestial ice enters the Earth's atmosphere and burns up. Meteors are small pieces of dust and ice that have previously evaporated from the tail of a comet that happened to pass near the Earth.

Comets are fun to observe either with the naked eye, binoculars, or telescopes. When they are far from the Sun, comets are invisible and resemble 20-kilometer (12-mile) dirty snowballs. As a comet approaches the Sun on an elongated, egg-shaped orbit, some of its frozen material melts and evaporates. Pushed by the pressure of sunlight, cometary vapor and dust often form one or more beautiful tails 100 million kilometers (60 million miles) in length during a comet's rare visit to the inner solar system.

Most of the asteroids lurk between the orbits of Mars and Jupiter. Some of these minor planets sometimes venture into the inner solar system. If a small asteroid survives the passage through the Earth's atmosphere and reaches our planet, it is called a *meteorite*. Some meteorites have been located by expeditions to remote corners of the Earth; others have been discovered by alert amateur astronomers in their backyards!

At around 7 P.M. on August 31, 1991, Brodie Spaulding (age 13) and Brian Kinzie (age 9) were chatting outdoors. They heard a strange, low-pitched whistle and then a thud. Brodie walked a few feet and found a small, fresh, warm meteorite sitting in a crater a few inches deep. The two discoverers, somewhat shaken by the near miss, contacted scientists who analyzed (and later returned) the stone.

Beyond the Solar Sea

Modern astronomers share the ancient delight in the constellations—those patterns of stars that grace the night sky. Along with being impressed by their beauty, you'll learn about the practical aspects of constellations. Once you can recognize them, they'll become landmarks in the sky.

But it's when you point your telescope at the individual points of light, or stars, that you will begin to really appreciate the immensity and diversity of the universe. It takes light about four years to travel from the Sun to our nearest stellar neighbor.

Our Sun and more than 100,000 million other stars are members of a vast spiral-shaped star city, or galaxy, called the Milky Way. During the summer, from a dark site, you can look toward the center of our galaxy. Although the eye cannot resolve, or separate, the millions of stars in these enormous star fields, your telescope can do the job easily.

Your telescope will make dim stars visible, as well as present the beautiful colors of the stars. Some of them will look like red or blue gemstones through your eyepiece; others will look yellow-white like the Sun. Blue stars are hotter and younger than our Sun; red stars are cooler and often much older.

During the winter, you'll observe through your telescope the blue-green Orion Nebula, where baby stars are forming. In the summer, you'll be able to observe the Great Spiral Galaxy in Andromeda, a near twin of our Milky Way, about two million light-years away.

PART 1
★ ★ ★

Understanding Your Telescope

★ ★ ★

★ 1 ★

The Telescope in History

E ven very early people, who had no telescopes, had an interest in the skies. Most of these ancients were not interested in performing scientific observations and measurements of the Sun, Moon, planets, and stars. Instead, they were viewing gods and goddesses, divine or semidivine beings who circled the Earth daily and who, they believed, could directly influence the lives of humans.

The Earliest Astronomers

In Africa and Europe, archaeologists have found animal bones on which humans carved symbols more than 10,000 years ago. Some of these symbols look like early attempts at accounting; others resemble crude attempts to record the phases of the Moon.

Why were these hunter/gatherers interested in the waxing and waning of the Earth's one natural satellite? Perhaps they were fascinated by the beauty of the night sky as they sat around the camp fire enjoying a meal after a successful hunt. Perhaps they were interested in the regularity of the lunar phase cycles and used it for some practical purpose.

More than 5,000 years ago, late Stone Age farmers began to construct an enormous ring of huge stones in what is now the British countryside near the city of Salisbury. Called Stonehenge, this now-ruined "temple" is believed by many modern scholars to have had astronomical applications. Through openings in stone circles, ancient priest/astronomers could have viewed the midsummer and midwinter sunrise and sunset, using the changing positions of the Moon and Sun to gauge the best time for planting and harvesting crops. Some

Stonehenge

people argue that Stonehenge could also have been an early "computer" for keeping track of the cycle of lunar eclipses.

How the Constellations and Planets Got Their Names

Patterns in the sky were a natural. Because they were easy to recognize and rose regularly when the skies were clear, the early civilizations around the Mediterranean Sea began to name these star groupings. The familiar grouping we call Orion the Hunter was an Egyptian Pharaoh to ancient Egyptians and the great hero Gilgamesh to people living in the early cities of the country now called Iraq. What we call the Big Dipper was variously referred to as the "Great Plough" by ancient Europeans and the "Big Bear" (Ursae Majoris) by ancient Asians and American Indians. More than 3,000 years ago, ships were guided using sightings of the Pleiades, a star grouping that was originally called the "Seven Sisters."

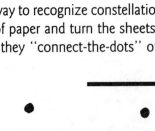 ACTIVITY
Recognizing Constellations

Look at the accompanying illustration of a familiar star pattern. Do you recognize it? If not, try holding the book upside down. Now you'll probably recognize this pattern as the Big Dipper.

One way to recognize constellations in any orientation is to draw the star patterns on sheets of paper and turn the sheets sideways and upside down. Some people also find that if they "connect-the-dots" of a constellation, they'll remember that pattern better.

Around the same time, people in Mesopotamia began to study the motions of mysterious objects that they called the "wanderers," which are now recognized as the naked-eye planets Mercury, Venus, Mars, Jupiter, and Saturn. These people were the first astrologers, believing that sky objects could intervene in terrestrial affairs. Far above the lights of their Bronze Age cities, at the summits of towers called Ziggurats, these scholars charted the motions of the naked-eye planets. (The most famous of the long-collapsed Ziggurats was immortalized in the Old Testament story of the Tower of Babel.)

 ACTIVITY
Planets in Motion

Here's how you can see planets move. First, get a star chart from a magazine, newspaper, or one of the sky manuals listed in Appendix C of this book, or purchase a star wheel at a local planetarium or hobby shop. These devices tell you what objects you can see in the evening sky during various seasons of the year. Your local newspaper may also have a "Sky Column" that will tell you what's going on in the sky that night.

From these charts, tables, and finders, you will learn which of the naked-eye planets can be observed. If you go out while Venus is an Evening Star, you will see it shortly after sunset. Venus usually outshines all celestial objects, other than the Moon and Sun.

On a clear evening, try to sketch the relative positions of Venus and the stars near it in the sky. Repeat your sky sketches at intervals of days or weeks, and you should be able to see the shifts in this planet's location, relative to the stationary stars near it (see illustrations).

Someone in ancient Mesopotamia had the idea to associate the planets with various gods and goddesses. Mercury, the closest planet to the Sun, changes its position rapidly as it revolves around the Sun in its 88-day orbit. Because of its speed, ancient astrologers identified this planet with the messenger of the gods.

Beautiful Venus, often the most brilliant object in our sky (after the Sun and Moon), is sometimes an Evening Star and sometimes a Morning Star. Because of this "fickle" nature and its brilliance and beauty, this planet became identified with the ancient goddess of love.

Mars, dimmer than Venus but still brighter than most stars, shines with a reddish hue. To the Mesopotamian astrologers, this red color was blood, and the planet was named after the ancient war god.

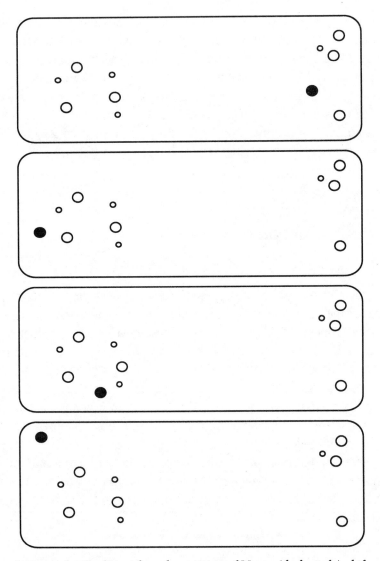

At intervals of a few nights, the position of Venus (dark circle) shifts against the background of fixed stars (open circles).

Jupiter, which orbits the Sun every 12 years, is by far the largest planet in our solar system. The ancient astrologers believed this brilliant planet to be the king of the gods.

Of the naked-eye planets, Saturn is the most distant from the Sun. It takes 25 years for Saturn to circle the Sun, which may be why this world was considered to be the ancient god of time.

Now that the ancient astrologers had decided which planet was associated with which god, it was necessary to come up with an efficient system of keeping track of these holy objects' motions. This was done by charting planet positions relative to familiar star patterns, or constellations.

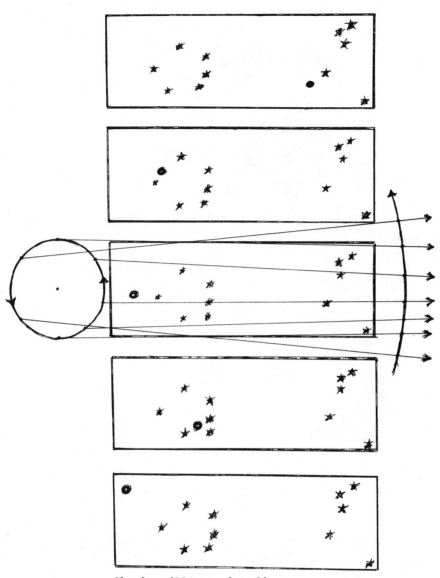

Sketches of Venus and neighboring stars

The Sun and naked-eye planets remain along the same track in the sky as their positions change with the seasons. This track is called the *ecliptic*. The 12 constellations near the ecliptic were of special interest to the ancient astrologers. These are the constellations or "houses" of the zodiac—Aries, Taurus, Gemini, Cancer, Leo, Virgo, Libra, Scorpio, Sagittarius, Capricorn, Aquarius, and Pisces. (You'll learn how to locate some of these with your telescope in Chapter 6).

According to the astrologers, the influence of the wandering "gods," the Moon, and the Sun depends upon one's birth date and the houses of the zodiac occupied by the various solar system objects. Astrological charts called *horo-*

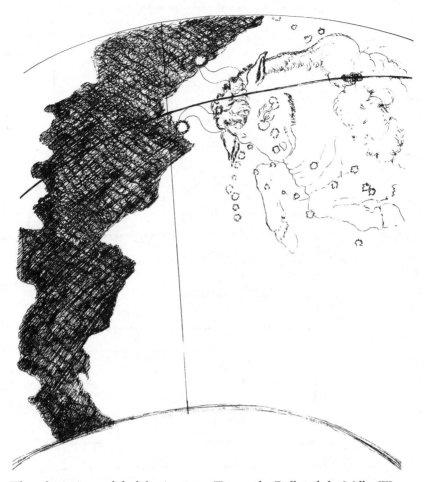

The ecliptic (curved dark line) crosses Taurus the Bull and the Milky Way.

scopes were cast by the Chaldeans and their followers in attempts to predict future events. Some people still believe in this today, although there is no scientific basis for astrology.

The First True Astronomers

As the power of Babylon waned, a new intellectual force arose in the ancient world. Approximately 500 B.C. (before the birth of Christ), Greek philosophers were developing a revolutionary method of viewing the universe.

Instead of believing in the power of supernatural sky gods, the Greek philosophers put their faith in the powers of the human mind. Starting from general principles and basic observations, they used logical reasoning to construct mental models of how the solar system might be constructed. Three different models of the solar system were developed.

In the *geocentric* (Earth-centered) solar system, the Earth was stationary at the center of the universe. The Moon, naked-eye planets, and Sun moved around the Earth in paths that were perfectly circular. "Fixed" stars—those celestial objects that seemed to pretelescopic observers to be unmoving points of light—were fastened to a crystal sphere beyond the orbit of Saturn, the most distant naked-eye planet from the Sun.

Many philosopher/astronomers worked out the details of the geocentric model over a period of almost a thousand years. Some who contributed were Aristotle, Ptolemy, and Hypatia, who was one of the first-known female astronomers.

As an alternative approach, the *heliocentric* (Sun-centered) model of the solar system was also a Greek invention. In this mathematical model, the planets circled the Sun and the Moon circled the Earth. The Sun was stationary in the center of the universe, and the Earth was assigned the position of third planet from the Sun—with Mercury and Venus closer to the Sun, and Mars, Jupiter, and Saturn more distant. As in the geocentric model, the fixed stars were attached to a crystal sphere and all planetary paths were circular.

A *compromise* solar system model, favored by the great pretelescopic astronomer Tycho Brahe, put the stationary Earth at the center. The Earth was circled by the Moon and Sun. This approach differed from the geocentric model in that the naked-eye planets still revolved around the Sun.

Other than Tycho Brahe, the compromise world view had few believers. Most astronomers considered the geocentric model to be correct until Copernicus proved the validity of the heliocentric model in the sixteenth century A.D.

 ACTIVITIES
Why Do Planets Sometimes Seem to Move Backward?

It is easy to picture how motions of the Earth and planets affect the apparent positions of the planets in the sky. Here are three simple activities that may help you understand such relative motions.

1. When you are a passenger in an automobile on a four-lane highway, observe motions of cars in the different lanes. If you are initially in the slow lane, look what happens when the driver shifts lanes and accelerates to pass a slow-moving vehicle. As you pass it, the slower vehicle seems to be moving backward, even though you are both moving forward.

2. This activity requires a pencil, a large sheet of paper, a compass, and two coins or other place markers. Using the compass, draw two circles on the paper, one about twice the size of the other, around the same center. The center of the circles represents our Sun. The small circle is the orbit of the Earth, and the large circle is the orbit of Mars. Divide each circle in half by drawing a line through the center and through the circle. Continue subdividing the circles until each has eight equal divisions (see illustration).

Number each division sequentially, starting with 0 and ending with 7. Place one marker or coin on the Earth's orbit at point 0 and one at point 0 on Mars's orbit. Draw a line between these points. If you were standing on the Earth, the projection of this line would correspond to the starting position of Mars in your sky.

Mars takes about twice as long as the Earth to complete one circuit around the Sun (or one orbit). Move the Mars marker to point 1 on Mars's orbit. The Earth marker must be moved to point 2 on the Earth's orbit. Once again, draw a line between the positions of the Earth and Mars. This line represents the position of Mars in the Earth's sky about one-fourth of an Earth-year (91 days) after the start of the activity.

Continue to draw a line between the positions of the Earth and Mars as you move

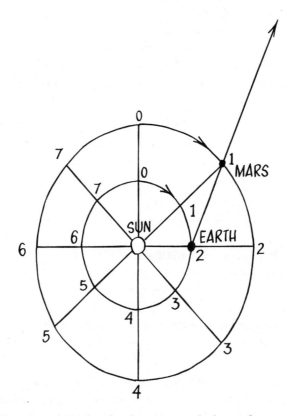

The planets Mars and Earth orbit the sun in a clockwise direction in this drawing. Both planets start at point 0. Mars moves to point 1 in the time it takes Earth to move to point 2. The arrow between Earth at point 2 and Mars at point 1 projects the position of Mars according to an observer on Earth at that time. Continue around the circle and see why Mars sometimes seems to go backward against the background stars.

your markers around the circles: when the Earth marker is at point 4 and the Mars marker is at point 2; when the Earth is at point 6 and Mars is at point 3; and, finally, when the Earth is back to the starting point at point 0 and Mars is at point 4.

When you examine the lines between the Earth and Mars, you will notice that the apparent position of Mars does not shift evenly between measurements. Sometimes the planet seems to speed up, sometimes it seems to slow down.

3. This activity is best performed with the assistance of a few friends in a meadow or park on a bright summer day. This time, use string to outline two circles centered on the same stone or tree (representing the Sun). One circle should be larger than the other. You, representing the Earth, should walk around the inner circle while your friend, "Mars," walks around the outer circle at about half your speed. You'll see how "Mars" seems to speed up, slow down, and even occasionally go backward!

Astronomical Celebrities

While Europe stagnated in the Dark Ages after the fall of the Roman Empire, Islamic scholars constructed magnificent naked-eye observatories at a number of locations. During the thirteenth and fourteenth centuries, observations made at these observatories began to percolate into Western Europe. In order

to explain the new observations of planetary motions, it was necessary to modify the old models. The geocentric model was becoming very, very complicated.

Nicholas Copernicus

Copernicus, perhaps the greatest Polish astronomer of all time, was born in 1473. While working as a Roman Catholic church canon, Copernicus rediscovered the heliocentric solar system model of the ancient Greeks, which had been ignored through the Dark Ages. After mathematically investigating both the geocentric and the heliocentric models, Copernicus showed that the heliocentric model explained the Islamic observations better than the geocentric model did.

It took a long time for scientists and other scholars to decide between the geocentric and heliocentric models. Finally, after centuries of debate, the heliocentric view of the solar system won general acceptance, largely because of the invention of the telescope. With some modifications, this view is still in use today.

Tycho Brahe

Perhaps the greatest of the pretelescopic astronomers was the colorful Danish nobleman Tycho Brahe (1546–1601). After his precise observations of the Supernova (exploding star) of 1572, Tycho's reputation as an observer was assured. The Danish monarch Frederik II granted Tycho possession of the island

A Swashbuckling Dane

At the age of 19 or 20, Tycho Brahe had a violent dispute with another young Danish nobleman regarding a mathematical problem. The two rivals were separated by friends before blows were exchanged. A week later, they met at a Christmas party. Undoubtedly under the influence of alcohol, the two drew their swords. During the duel, Tycho's nose was neatly snipped off! For the rest of his life, this vain and arrogant astronomer would wear a silver nose painted to resemble flesh.

If the great observer's life was colorful, his reported manner of death is perhaps even more unique. One of Tycho's noble duties was to occasionally attend royal banquets. On October 13, 1601, while at the table of Baron Rosenberg of Prague, an aging Tycho consumed a fair amount of alcoholic beverage. Because it was considered poor etiquette to leave the table before his host, Tycho maintained his seat and composure under growing discomfort. Within 11 days he would die of a burst bladder—an undignified end for this nobleman of the heavens.

Tycho's strange theory of planet motion was as far off base as his swordsmanship!

of Hveen. On Hveen, Tycho constructed Uraniborg—the world's finest naked-eye observatory.

True to his noble stock, Tycho ruled Uraniborg as a feudal fiefdom. Along with running water and well-equipped laboratories, the observatory even had a jail!

Perhaps Tycho used the threat of imprisonment to drive his assistants to make ever-more accurate measurements of planetary positions. He devoted much of his professional life in a vain attempt to prove the compromise model of the solar system—that all the planets except Earth circled the Sun. The Sun and Moon, in turn, circled a stationary Earth.

Tycho employed many of the most talented mathematicians in Europe in his effort to prove his strange view of the solar system. Foremost among these was his last mathematical assistant—the brilliant but quirky Johannes Kepler.

Johannes Kepler

Kepler's mathematical collaboration with Tycho Brahe began eighteen months before Tycho's death in 1601. As the last—and probably greatest—of Tycho's mathematical assistants, Kepler was able to "inherit" Tycho's vast store of planetary observations. Using this data, particularly Tycho's meticulous observations of the motions of Mars, Kepler was able to formulate the Laws of Elliptical Planetary Motion—which helped explain the motions of the planets.

According to Kepler, all the planets circled the Sun in elliptical (or egg-shaped) orbits, rather than in circular paths. Planets sped up when they were closer to the Sun and slowed down when they were most distant from the Sun. In addition, Kepler discovered a mathematical relationship between a planet's period of revolution around the Sun (or *year*) and its average distance from the Sun.

Galileo Galilei

A member of a noble but impoverished Italian family, Galileo was born in 1564. After successfully applying the telescope—a Dutch invention originally used as a terrestrial "spy glass"—to astronomy, he attempted to establish telescopic astronomy as an exclusive monopoly. He certainly succeeded in a sense. Even today, many people believe that Galileo invented the telescope.

Although Galileo did not invent the telescope, he was certainly the first to apply it to astronomy. With it, he observed many astronomical wonders including features on the Moon, the four large satellites of Jupiter, and sunspots. Galileo enthusiastically reported his observational discoveries to the largest audience he could reach.

Galileo believed in the heliocentric view of the solar system, which at the time was considered a heresy by the Roman Catholic church. In 1633, he was called before the Inquisition in Rome. When threatened with some of the ingenious instruments of torture (including the infamous rack), the old man agreed to recant his heretical Copernican views.

For the last three years of his life, he continued his research under house arrest, even though he was sick and essentially blind (as a result of his direct viewing of the Sun through the telescope). Galileo died on January 8, 1642. Perhaps the greatest physical scientist of all time, Isaac Newton, was born on December 25 of that year.

Sir Isaac Newton

The premature and sickly child of a rural English family, Newton was not fit for the farmer's role. He felt unloved by his parents and was far from sociable. In addition to his scientific contributions, Newton was interested in astrology, mysticism, alchemy, and scriptural interpretation.

The famous story of how Sir Isaac deduced the Law of Universal Gravitation when he noticed an apple fall in an orchard as he was staring at the Moon is legendary, but the truth is just as remarkable.

A fellow scientist, Edmund Halley, goaded Newton with the possibility that a competitor, Robert Hooke, would beat him to the mathematical proof of universal gravitation. Sufficiently aroused, Newton recreated calculations that he had first performed in 1666 and somehow lost!

Halley himself became a world famous figure because he was able to use Newton's calculations to predict the return of the celestial spectacle that we now call Halley's comet.

Newton also contributed to the further development of the telescope. One commonly used telescope, the Newtonian reflector, is based upon his research in optics that led to replacing telescope lenses with mirrors.

Telescopic Astronomy after Newton

After the work of Sir Isaac Newton, there was no going back. The modern world was here to stay. And foremost among the tools of the new scientists was the telescope. Astronomers were soon peering farther into space with their new instruments. They charted the paths of the planets and the features of planetary atmospheres and surfaces with increasing accuracy. They named and cataloged the mountains, craters, and plains of our Moon, discovered moons circling many of the other solar system worlds, and demonstrated that the stars are not points of light on a crystal sphere, but incredibly distant objects like our Sun. In the twentieth century, astronomers have learned that the stars, including our Sun, cluster in enormous star groups called *galaxies*. Now, with advanced telescopes on Earth and in space, they are probing toward the very edges of the universe.

During the last three centuries, telescopic technology has improved steadily. Telescopic designers have learned to craft better lenses and mirrors, to fold the optical paths of reflectors, and to reduce the size of these devices. The invention of electricity has allowed for the construction of *clock drives*, devices that automatically move a telescope to follow the stars. This allows astronomers to photograph the stars.

As you observe the heavens with your telescope, you will join hands with many of the great minds of astronomy—people like Edwin Hubble (who demonstrated early in the twentieth century that the universe was expanding) and Jill Tarter (a leading radio astronomer who conducts searches for signals from intelligent aliens).

The telescope will stretch your mind in the same way that it has enlarged the vistas of civilization. No longer content to dream of a stationary Earth in the center of a small, unchanging cosmos, you will experience an infinite universe.

★ 2 ★
How Your Telescope Works

Your telescope can show you wonderful things and take you incredible distances across the universe. To understand it, you must know that a telescope is a "creature of light."

Light is the medium of vision, one of the most important of the five senses (vision, hearing, touch, smell, and taste) that we use to gather information about our environment. On a clear night, some of the light from the heavens will reach your telescope, and your telescope will "process" this light to direct an image to your eye. Here's how that light works.

Light: The Signature of the Universe

Visible light is a form of energy called *electromagnetic* (or E-M) *radiation* (which also includes invisible energy, such as radio waves and X rays). Unlike other forms of E-M radiation, our eyes recognize only visible light.

Light moves in waves, something like ocean waves. Stand on the shoreline with a stopwatch and time the number of waves that reach the shore every second. If one wave reaches the shore every second, the *wave frequency* is one wave per second. Next, stand in the surf with a yardstick and try to measure the distance between a wave crest and the crest of the wave following it. This distance is called the *wavelength*.

You'll notice that the ocean waves move toward you from the deep ocean. The rate at which waves approach you is called *wave velocity*. Water, sound, and light waves all have different wave velocities.

A simple formula relates the wavelength, frequency, and velocity of a wave. If you multiply the frequency (in waves per second) by the wavelength (in feet), you'll obtain the wave velocity (in feet per second).

Near the shore, water waves usually move at a few miles per hour. In the near vacuum of deep space, light gallops along at an astounding 300,000 kilometers (186,000 miles) per second! In denser mediums, such as your telescope's glass eyepiece lens, light slows down to about 200,000 kilometers (125,000 miles) per second.

The basic unit of E-M radiation is called the *photon*. High-frequency photons have smaller wavelengths than low-frequency photons. A high-frequency *gamma ray* or an X-ray photon can be thought of as a small, compact, and very energetic bullet. This is why your doctor and dentist use X rays to learn what goes on inside your body. The high-energy, high-frequency X ray passes through most human tissue, being stopped only by bone. Gamma rays have even higher energy than X rays.

The next less energetic form of E-M radiation after X rays is *ultraviolet light*. Ultraviolet light can penetrate only the outermost skin layers. Sun blocks can be used to protect skin from the damaging ultraviolet light from the Sun.

Rays of visible light have less energy than ultraviolet light. Less energetic than visible light is that band of the spectrum called the *infrared*. Infrared radiation does not penetrate human skin. It is sensed as heat.

The least energetic kinds of E-M radiation, those with the longest wavelengths, are microwaves and television and radio waves. Like infrared light, these waves are not energetic enough to penetrate human skin.

How Does the Light from Space Originate?

All of the different types of light (visible and invisible) are energy. No matter what their wavelength and frequency, all of the photons traveling through space have a common origin.

Deep inside all stars (including our Sun), pressures and temperatures are high enough that hydrogen atoms can be forced together, or *fused*. In this *thermonuclear reaction*, a small fraction of the mass of reacting particles is converted into energy. This energy comes out in the form of gamma rays.

As the gamma rays rise toward the star's surface, they react with various atoms in the star's interior. By the time the photons reach the star's surface, much of the thermonuclear energy originally in the form of gamma rays has been converted through these reactions into X rays, ultraviolet light, visible light, and the other forms of light in the E-M spectrum.

Light in the Earth's Atmosphere

After escaping from the Sun (or another star), a light photon streaks through space at 300,000 kilometers (186,000 miles) per second. It may reach your eyes directly, or it may be reflected from the surface of a planet or satellite.

When a stream of photons strikes our planet's atmosphere, a number of things happen. Some of the photons are immediately reflected into space by the Earth's atmosphere. Atoms in the Earth's upper atmosphere (the *ionosphere*) remove most of the gamma rays and X rays from the photon stream by absorbing them.

About 20 kilometers (12 miles) above the surface of the Earth is an atmospheric layer known as the *stratosphere*. In the stratosphere, most of the ultraviolet light photons are absorbed by an unusual form of oxygen called *ozone*. In recent years, an increasing number of people have become concerned about possible deterioration of the ozone layer. If the ozone layer continues to disappear, the increased amount of ultraviolet rays reaching the ground will make a summer visit to the beach hazardous to your health!

Most of the Earth's water vapor is in the lowest atmospheric layer, called the *troposphere*. Here, just above the ground, water vapor and a gas called carbon dioxide absorb most of the infrared radiation.

Of all the photons that enter the Earth's atmosphere, almost all the gamma rays, X rays, ultraviolet light, and infrared radiation are blocked by the Earth's atmosphere. On the other hand, most of the visible light and radio wave photons reach the Earth's surface. These two regions of the E-M spectrum are called the *atmospheric windows* by astronomers.

In the lowest portion of the atmosphere, some of the visible light photons are *scattered*, or reflected, by atmospheric gases. Because blue photons are more easily scattered than red photons, the sky is blue when viewed from the Earth's surface. From the viewpoint of astronauts above the atmosphere, the sky is black.

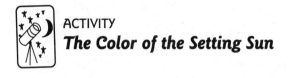

ACTIVITY
The Color of the Setting Sun

You can get a good feel for the variable-scattering effect of the Earth's atmosphere by observing the color changes of the Sun as it sets. By glancing indirectly in the direction of the Sun when it is high in the sky, you have of course noticed our star's predominant yellow color. As the Sun sets, its light travels through more of the Earth's atmosphere and therefore is more affected by scattering. This is why the Sun seems redder just before it sets (or after it rises) than when it is higher in the sky.

Of course the blue photons scattered by the atmosphere don't just disappear. At the same time that scattering makes the Sun "redder," the day sky gets "bluer."

But even those photons that reach the Earth's surface are not unaffected by their passage through the Earth's atmosphere. When light leaves one medium and enters another (say from space into air, or air into water), its velocity changes and its path is bent, or *refracted*. Light slows down as it goes from space into air; it slows again if it enters water or glass.

ACTIVITIES
Observing Refraction

One way of observing refraction is to pitch coins into an aquarium or a swimming pool. The trajectory (or path) of a coin seems to change when it enters the water. If you have an aquarium, notice how a fish's position seems to change when it is viewed from above and from the side.

If you have a good sky view to the western (or eastern) horizon, you might be able to observe the setting (or rising) Sun. Notice how the Sun's image seems to spread out from a sphere into a "blob" when it is close to the horizon. This effect occurs because light from the part of the Sun near the Earth's horizon travels through more atmosphere than light from the parts of the Sun that are higher in the sky. Light rays near the horizon experience more bending by refraction.

Kinds of Telescopes

Refractors

A *refractor* is a telescope that uses lenses alone to magnify objects. It is a modern version of the first astronomical telescopes used by Galileo. The large *objective lens* collects light from a distant object and delivers this light beam to the *eyepiece*, the lens or set of lenses at the back of the tube. The eyepiece then focuses the light on your eye. If the image is properly focused and the optics are properly aligned, you will observe a bright and distinct image of the celestial object.

Reflectors

A Newtonian *reflector*, the earliest type of reflecting telescope, uses lenses only in the eyepiece. Most of the work is done by mirrors. Light is collected by a curved *primary mirror*. A flat *secondary mirror*, which is much smaller than the primary mirror, directs the collected light to the eyepiece.

Early reflectors were large and hard to work with. In 1672, an obscure Frenchman named N. Cassegrain designed a reflecting telescope with a curved secondary mirror. Many large and small modern telescopes use Cassegrain's approach to bend the light further. These telescopes are more compact than many Newtonians of the same primary mirror diameter.

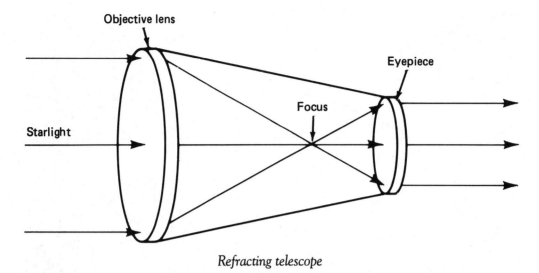

Refracting telescope

Catadioptic (Schmidt–Cassegrain) Telescopes

Many telescopes are affected by problems in the optical system called *aberrations*. Optical designers can correct aberrations by carefully selecting the glass(es) of which the optical lenses are constructed. On some reflectors, this is done by adding another refractive element, called a *correcting lens*, at the entrance to the telescope tube. Such a hybrid telescope, which combines elements of a reflector and a refractor, is called a *catadioptic telescope*. An example of a catadioptic telescope that is used by both amateur and professional astronomers is the Schmidt–Cassegrain.

All astronomical telescopes invert the image (turn it upside down). So if you look at a terrestrial scene through your telescope, the image will be upside down! Binoculars, a type of refractor that can be used by both eyes at the same time, use a prism or some other optical component to "reinvert" the image so that it looks right side up.

Terms You Should Know

All sky-viewing devices (binoculars, refracting telescopes, reflecting telescopes, and catadioptic telescopes) have three basic functions. First, they enhance the *light-gathering power* of the human eye to make dim objects appear brighter. Second, they *magnify*, make larger, small objects. Third, a good telescope or pair of binoculars will *resolve*, or make clearer, details on distant or dim objects—details invisible to the naked eye.

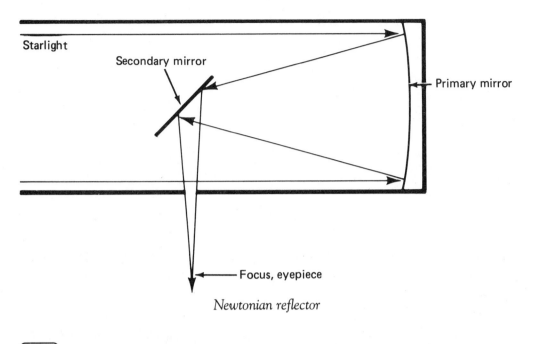

Starlight

Secondary mirror

Primary mirror

Focus, eyepiece

Newtonian reflector

ACTIVITY
Boresighting Your Telescope

Many telescopes are equipped with a small *finder scope*. The finder scope can be used as a first step in centering a celestial object in the telescope's eyepiece. The magnification of the finder scope is less than that of the main telescope.

It may be necessary to *boresight*, or align, your finder scope and main telescope before you try to observe distant celestial objects. Be sure to read the instructions supplied by the telescope's manufacturer.

Then go outside during the day. Point the instrument at a distant terrestrial object—a flagpole or smokestack, for example. Locate the image in the center of the finder scope.

Next, make sure that you have the lowest magnification eyepiece in place on the telescope. Observe the distant flagpole or smokestack through the telescope. (Don't be alarmed that the telescope image is upside down. This is normal for most telescopes.) Adjust the alignment of the telescope and finder scope until the image is centered in both the finder scope and the telescope eyepiece.

Repeat the process for the next highest eyepiece magnification. While you are boresighting your telescope, you should practice changing eyepieces without moving the telescope so that at night, when observing a celestial object, you will be able to change eyepieces easily by feel without upsetting the pointing direction. Once you've found your celesial object you won't want to lose it just because you've bumped the telescope!

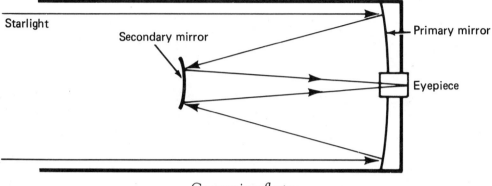

Cassegrain reflector

Before examining these three basic functions in detail, take a look at your telescope's insides. If you have a refractor (or binoculars), look at the largest lens—the one farthest from the eye. This is called the *objective lens* and defines the *aperture*. The aperture of a reflector is equal to the size of the largest, or primary, mirror. The size of these optical elements is found by measuring the diameter (an imaginary line crossing the lens or mirror through the center).

It's not a good idea to try to measure your telescope's aperture, because it's very easy to scratch a lens or mirror or to disturb the optical alignment. Instead, read your telescope owner's manual for details on the instrument's aperture.

Light-gathering Power

The *pupil* of the eye is the variable-aperture opening in the center of the eyeball. In bright light, the pupil contracts so that its diameter is about 0.2 centimeter (less than 0.1 inch); in dim light (such as starlight), it expands to almost 1 centimeter (0.4 inch) in diameter. In bright light, the eyes are called *light adapted;* at night, the eyes are *dark adapted.* To see the change in pupil size, look at your eyes in the bathroom mirror with a bright light on. Then turn off the light, making sure there's a little light coming in from the hallway. Watch your pupil expand as it adapts to less light.

If your telescope has an objective lens or primary mirror of 10 centimeters (4 inches) in diameter, its aperture is also 4 inches (10 centimeters). This is a bit more than ten times the aperture of the typical dark-adapted human eye.

To compare the light-gathering power of your telescope and your eye, think of rain falling vertically into an open barrel. The amount of rain collected by the barrel depends upon the area of the barrel's opening. A rain barrel with a 10-centimeter (4-inch) diameter opening has 100 times the area of a rain barrel with a 1-centimeter (0.4-inch) opening (because the area of the circular barrel depends upon the diameter multiplied by itself). Therefore, the 10-centimeter (4-inch) barrel will gather 100 times more rainwater than a 1-centi-

A Sidewalk Astronomer

Not all people who have made significant contributions to telescopic astronomy were schooled in the subject. One recent telescopic innovation was the development of a new type of Newtonian reflector by John L. Dobson.

You could not have predicted Dobson's contribution from his upbringing and early training. The son of a zoologist and a missionary's daughter, Dobson was born in China. His academic training was in chemistry.

After moving to the United States, Dobson joined a monastery in San Francisco. He took up astronomy as a hobby during the 1950s and began to experiment with Newtonian telescopes constructed from scrap materials, such as cardboard, hose reels, and war-surplus glass.

Dobson constructed Newtonian telescopes with apertures of 30 centimeters (12 inches) and larger. The telescopes were constructed with hollow tubes and mounted on wheels, in order to cut costs and weight. These early "Dobsonians" were portable enough to be pulled around the city and mounted in various urban neighborhoods. As a result, many children (and their parents) were introduced to astronomy by John Dobson and his merry band of "sidewalk astronomers."

Since leaving the monastery, Dobson has devoted his full attention to sidewalk astronomy. In a recent book—J. L. Dodson, *How and Why to Make a User-Friendly Sidewalk Telescope*, N. Sperling, ed. (Oakland, CA: Everything in the Universe, 1991)—he reveals some of the secrets behind his easy-to-construct and inexpensive telescopic design.

meter barrel, providing both are exposed to the rainstorm for the same length of time.

Similarly, your 10-centimeter (4-inch) aperture telescope will gather 100 times more light from a distant star or planet than the human eye will. Objects in the sky will seem 100 times brighter when viewed through a telescope than through your unassisted eye. Light-gathering power is the same as light amplification.

 ACTIVITY
Rain Buckets and Light Buckets

You can gain a good feel for your telescope's light-gathering power by performing a simple experiment on a rainy day. Take two kitchen glasses of different diameters.

Take the two glasses outside, and place them side-by-side where they are exposed to the rain. While they are filling with rainwater, find two other (transparent) containers of equal size.

John Dobson constructs a reflecting telescope.

Leave the two glasses outside until a small column of water has collected in each of them. This may take a few hours, unless it's raining very hard.

After sufficient rainwater has been gathered, take your two "rain buckets" back inside. First compare the heights of the water columns in these two unequal rain buckets. The heights will be equal.

Pour the contents of each into one of the two transparent containers of equal size. Once again, compare the heights of the water columns. The height of the water column from the larger-diameter rain bucket will be greater, indicating that this bucket collected more water. You might want to try this using rain buckets of widely varying aperture, such as a glass and a thimble.

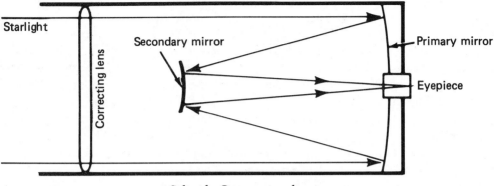

Schmidt–Cassegrain telescope

Magnification

Magnification measures image size. The magnification of a telescope is usually defined using the symbol X. A magnification of 35X means "35 times." To understand how magnification works, imagine that an insect ⅟₃₅ the length of this book is crawling on the table next to it. If you use an optical device to magnify the image of the insect by 35X, the insect will seem as long as the unmagnified book.

Magnification depends upon the *focal lengths* of the primary mirror or objective lens and the eyepiece. When you change to a lower, or shorter, focal-length eyepiece, the magnification of your telescope increases. The focal length of a lens can be found by pointing that lens at a distant light source. If you hold a sheet of paper up to the side of the lens farther from the light source, you'll notice a blurry image of the light source on the sheet of paper. Now move the sheet of paper back and forth. The image is in focus when the circle of light from the light source on the paper is the smallest. When the image is in focus, the focal length is the distance between the lens and paper.

On most telescope or binocular eyepieces, the focal length is given in millimeters (mm). A focal length of 50 mm is roughly equivalent to 2 inches.

ACTIVITY
Estimating Magnification

To get a feel for your telescope's magnification, compare the size of a distant object when viewed through the telescope and through the eye. With a refractor, you can do

Hubble: An Eye in the Sky

Because most of the nonvisible light from distant stars is stopped by the Earth atmosphere, astronomers have long wanted to use permanent observatories located in space. The largest of these to date, the Hubble space telescope, was launched by the space shuttle in 1990. This 2.4-meter (8-foot) aperture reflecting telescope was soon found to suffer from aberrations. A repair mission is planned.

Even with its optical limitations, this solar-powered space telescope has proven its worth. Hubble has returned excellent photographs and other data about nearby planets, stars, and galaxies billions of light-years from the Earth.

this by first looking through the eyepiece at a distant object with the other eye closed, and then looking at the object directly with the other (unaided) eye.

Point your telescope at a distant structure—a chimney, for example. Let's say that the telescope's magnification is 50X and that the structure is composed of about 50 bricks. Through the telescope, each brick will seem about as large as the whole structure does when viewed with the unaided eye.

If you switch to a higher-powered eyepiece, each brick through the telescope will seem larger than the entire structure does when viewed with the unaided eye.

Resolution

Resolution is a measure of image clarity. For example, assume you have two telescopes of identical magnifications, but one has better resolution than the other. The higher-resolution instrument will be better suited for showing the details of craters on the Moon or for separating the members of a binary star system.

Resolution (also called resolving power) depends upon a telescope's aperture. If all other factors are equal, a 10-centimeter (4-inch) aperture telescope will have twice the resolving power of a 5-centimeter (2-inch) telescope, and five times the resolution of a 2-centimeter (0.8 inch) telescope.

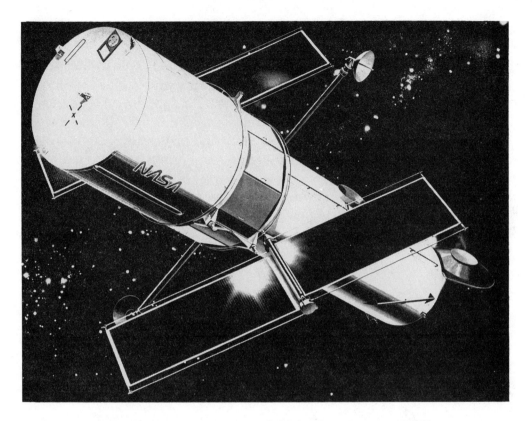

Like most large, modern telescopes, the 8-ft. 2.4-m aperture Hubble telescope is a reflector. (Courtesy NASA)

 ACTIVITY
Resolution versus Magnification

Magnification measures image size; resolution measures image clarity. To help you understand the difference between these two functions, find a distant terrestrial object, such as a tree. Point your telescope at the tree and view it under low magnification. Focus until you have a very clear image. Now carefully change to a shorter focal length eyepiece. Under higher magnification, you'll be able to see more detail on the tree.

Next, replace the original eyepiece and repeat the experiment with the low-magnification image slightly out of focus. Now when you change eyepieces, the higher magnification does not reveal more detail on the tree. The image is simply larger and less distinct.

Inexperienced telescope purchasers sometimes are taken in by claims of high magnification. High magnification on a low-aperture instrument is a rip-off because the images, though comparatively large, will be indistinct and blurry.

Field of View (FOV)

Telescopes are often compared using the term *field of view* (FOV). To understand the FOV of your telescope, stand outside on a clear evening. The spot in the sky directly above your head is called the *zenith*. The spot directly under your feet in the sky on the other side of the Earth is called the *nadir*. If you draw an imaginary circle that passes through the zenith and nadir, the circle will contain 360 degrees of arc, or 360°. The distance from horizon to horizon, a semicircle, contains 180 degrees. If your telescope has an FOV rating of 1 degree, this means that $\frac{1}{180}$ of the semicircle between horizons that passes through the zenith can be viewed at any one time through your telescope.

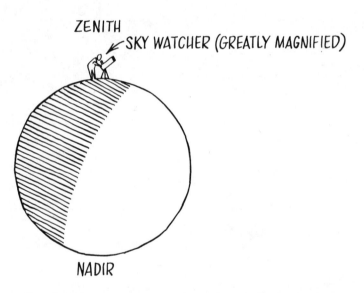

The zenith is the point in the sky directly overhead. The nadir is the point in the sky on the other side of the Earth on an imaginary line passing through the feet of the sky watcher.

The Care and Feeding of Your Telescope

By now, you're probably aware of how marvelous and sensitive a tool your telescope is. With a bit of common sense, this magnificent instrument will give you a lifetime of service.

Try not to touch your telescope's lenses or mirrors, and don't leave your instrument next to a radiator for a long time. The alignment of optical equipment is a precision art—so you should resist the temptation to take apart your telescope or its accessories.

You should clean the eyepieces as infrequently as possible and then only with special lens paper or a camel's-hair brush. You can get these inexpensive tools at many eyeglass stores or hobby shops. Lenses and mirrors should not be removed from their casing by inexperienced persons. If there's a problem with them, take the telescope to the manufacturer or an authorized repair shop.

It's a good idea to cover all lenses of a refractor or catadioptic telescope as well as reflector eyepieces with plastic covers when you're not using them. A Newtonian's primary mirror will be protected if you keep a dustcover over the telescope's aperture when the instrument is not in use.

Try not to jostle the telescope too much as you move it from place to place.

To prevent dew buildup on your telescope's optics, don't bring the instrument immediately from the cold outdoors into a warm room. It's a better idea to vary its temperature gradually. You might leave it for a while in your building vestibule or garage before moving the telescope indoors. If moisture from dew does appear on the lenses, let it dry gradually as the telescope adjusts to room temperature. Never rub a lens when it is damp.

★ 3 ★

Selecting Your Telescope and Its Accessories

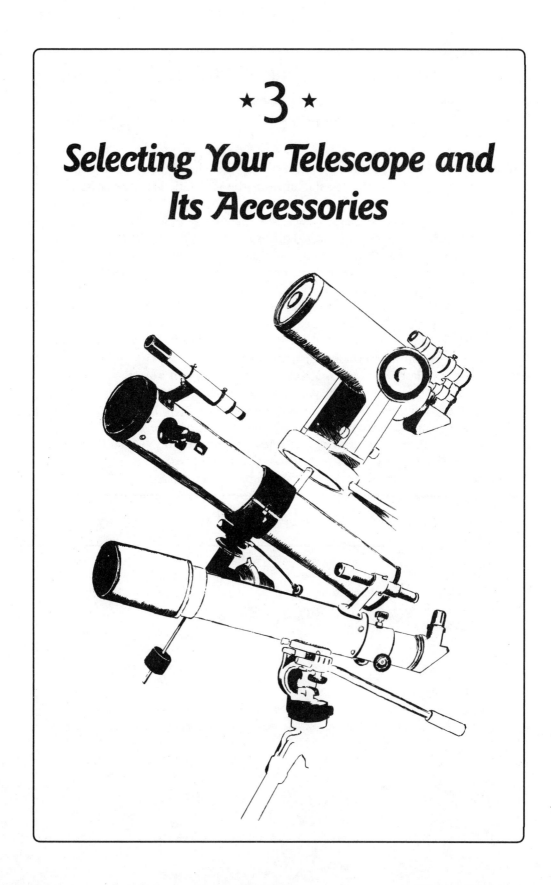

*I*f you glance through one of the popular astronomy magazines, *Odyssey* (for young astronomers), *Sky & Telescope*, or *Astronomy*, you may be surprised and a bit bewildered by the selection of telescopes and accessories available for purchase.

You'll see small telescopes, medium-sized telescopes, and very large telescopes. There are refracting telescopes and Newtonian and Dobsonian reflectors, as well as more compact reflectors. Telescopes come with different magnifications, resolutions, and fields of view (see Chapter 2 for descriptions of these terms). Some instruments have setting circles (devices that simplify the location of faint celestial objects); others have clock drives (electrical units that compensate for the Earth's daily rotation).

A wide variety of eyepieces, optical filters, and other accessories also exists. And to help you find your way among the stars, you might want to collect star charts, star finders, star atlases, or even astronomical computer software for a home computer.

In this chapter, you'll be introduced to some of the options available. In addition to price, you should think about what you want to be able to do with your telescope. Your astronomical experience will be greatly enhanced if you understand your telescope and its accessories.

Your Local Astronomy Club

One resource that can help you as your interest in astronomy develops is a local astronomy society or club. Many cities and towns have clubs of this type. Addresses and phone numbers of local astronomy clubs throughout the United States and Canada are listed in special "activity resource" issues of *Astronomy* and *Sky & Telescope* magazines. *Sky & Telescope* resource issues are usually published in September. The *Astronomy* activity supplement is often in the May issue. Another good source of information regarding astronomy clubs is your local planetarium or science museum.

If you decide to join an astronomy club, you'll enjoy participating in the group observing sessions, which are usually held in excellent observing locations and are very well attended. The more experienced astronomers can help you locate difficult-to-find celestial objects, and you'll be able to view the heavens through a wide variety of instruments. This can help you make a decision on what equipment you want to buy.

Many amateur astronomy clubs also feature telescope-making classes, lectures by expert astronomers, and other activities. Through the contacts you make at meetings of your local astronomy club, you also may be able to get a good deal on a used telescope or accessories.

Telescope Selection

Even if you have limited financial resources to devote to astronomy, you can purchase a reasonably good pair of binoculars (magnification 7X, field of view 7 degrees) or a low-field, low-magnification refractor for less than $100 in most department stores. With such an inexpensive instrument, you can begin your astronomical experience. You'll be able to see craters and other large features on the Moon's surface, keep track of the phases of Venus, and observe the large satellites of Jupiter and the rings of Saturn. Many more stars will be visible through such an instrument than can be seen with the unaided eye. But with a bit more money, you can purchase a superior instrument.

Newtonian Reflectors

When you shop for a Newtonian reflector, or any other telescope, the mount is almost as important as the optics. Some telescopes have *alt–az mounts*, which make it very easy for a novice astronomer to locate sky objects. But if you want to track a particular sky object as the Earth's rotation causes that object to move across the sky, an *equatorial mount* should be your choice.

One versatile type of Newtonian reflector with an alt–az mount is the wide-field Newtonian. It is of special value to the observer who requires a rugged instrument that can be easily taken to observing sites. Some of these instruments weigh less than 15 pounds (7 kilograms), have a field of view of 3 degrees, have an aperture of more than 10 centimeters (4 inches), and cost less than $400. The magnification for these instruments, however, tends to be less than 20X unless you purchase optional eyepieces or lenses.

A wide variety of less-portable and more expensive Newtonian reflectors are on the market. Generally, more capable instruments are both larger and more expensive.

If, however, you don't mind sacrificing portability and would still like a truly large and inexpensive Newtonian, one also on an alt–az mount, you might try a Dobsonian. Although this type of Newtonian reflector allows you to see many faint celestial objects, more expensive instruments of equal aperture will usually produce better images. In certain locations, the low-weight tube structure of some Dobsonians may also be more buffeted by winds than the tubes of more massive instruments.

For most viewing purposes, many astronomers prefer midsize Newtonian telescopes on equatorial mounts. Such telescopes are fairly portable and not too expensive. You can find a celestial object without too much difficulty and then track it across the sky. As aperture size increases, however, the portability of the Newtonian begins to suffer.

10
inches

This wide-field Newtonian and its alt–az mount are very portable and easy to use.

Catadioptic Telescopes

Catadioptic telescopes are very portable. They are more expensive than comparable-aperture Newtonians, but cheaper than high-quality refractors. Most catadioptic telescopes have equatorial mounts and excellent light-gathering power.

This type of telescope is particularly nice for viewing the delicate colors of dim celestial objects. It's not too difficult to mount a special camera on a catadioptic telescope and obtain beautiful color pictures of the Moon, planet, stars, and interstellar clouds of gas. The optical alignment of catadioptic telescopes is often more delicate than that of Newtonian reflectors.

Refractors

Refractors, which are somewhat more cumbersome, are often more expensive than reflectors of equal quality and aperture. If, however, you are bitten someday by the "astronomical photography bug," you may invest in a high-quality refractor with an equatorial mount.

Magnification

If your telescope is of reasonably good quality, a maximum magnification of 20 powers per centimeter (50 powers per inch) of aperture is an approximate esti-mate for maximum useful magnification. With a 7.5-centimeter (3-inch) ap-erture telescope, you could view productively using a magnification of 150X; a 15-centimeter (6-inch) aperture telescope will produce good images with a magnification of 300X.

Your location (urban, suburban, or rural) and the sky conditions will also influence the choice of optimum magnification. The chart below presents some recommendations for low, medium, and high magnifications for telescopes of various apertures. These shouldn't be accepted as hard-and-fast rules, but treated instead as useful guidelines.

Where to Buy Telescopes

Telescopes, binoculars, and other instruments are advertised each month in *Sky & Telescope* and *Astronomy* magazines. They are also available in department and hobby stores, and are marketed through special catalogs. The chart on the next page, which has been prepared from these sources, presents general price ranges for some telescope/binocular options. Further information on vendors of astronomical equipment is included in Appendix A.

Accessory Selection

Your first binocular or telescope purchase may not be your last purchase of astronomical equipment. You will probably wish to upgrade with equipment such as a reticle eyepiece (which allows you to measure the distances between

Magnification Recommendations for Telescopes of Various Apertures (Powers)

Telescope Aperture		Telescope Magnification		
Inches	Centimeters	Low	Medium	High
2	5	15	50	80
4	10	30	100	200
6	15	50	150	300
8	20	60	200	400

Price List for Selected Telescopes and Binoculars

Instrument	Approximate Price
wide-field Newtonian	
10-cm (4-in.) aperture	$300–$400
refractor, alt–az mount	
9-cm (3.6-in.) aperture	$600
8-cm (3.2-in.) aperture	$500
6-cm (2.4-in.) aperture	$169
catadioptic, equatorial mount, clock drive	
10-cm (4-in.) aperture	$600
Newtonian, 11-cm (4.5-in.) aperture	
alt–az mount	$300
equatorial mount	$400–$450
Dobsonian	
25-cm (10-in.) aperture	$345
20-cm (8-in.) aperture	$275
binoculars	
Magnification 7X, 7° FOV, 28-oz. weight	$80
Magnification 8X, 6° FOV, 33-oz. weight	$149

Note: A 1-ounce weight is equivalent to a mass of 0.028 kilogram.

or the apparent sizes of celestial objects), a wider selection of eyepieces, filters, clock drives, and star atlases. If you own a computer, you may wish to investigate the wide range of astronomical software available.

As with telescopes and binoculars, the price ranges of astronomical accessories is quite variable. The chart on the next page, used in conjunction with the vendor listing in Appendix A and manufacturer information advertised monthly in astronomy magazines, can help you learn about the cost and variety of optional accessories. Of course, you should take care to order accessories that are compatible with your equipment.

Eyepieces

Different eyepieces are appropriate for different viewing situations. As a general rule, an eyepiece with a long focal length will have a lower magnification and a larger field of view than an eyepiece with a short focal length.

For example, if you are observing the Moon or another large sky object, low magnification and large field of view are preferable because you want to view all of the object at the same time. Therefore, you'll probably want an eyepiece with a long focal length for lunar viewing.

On the other hand, a short focal length will bring out more details on the

Price List for Selected Accessories

Accessory	Approximate Price
clock drive	$100–$300
equatorial mount with setting circles	$200
eyepiece filters	
per filter	$12–$30
per set of 4	$45–$50
per set of 8	$85
per set of 12	$120
optional eyepieces	$35–$150
reticle eyepiece	$75–$150
solar aperture (ND) filter	$45–$220
software (for Macintosh and IBM technology)	$15–$200
star atlas	$20–$45
star wheel	$2.50

Note: The price of aperture filters will vary with your telescope's aperture.

surface of a distant planet. In such a case, high magnification is often more important than small field of view.

Many lunar observers center the entire Moon in the field of view with a low-magnification lens in place first and then change to a high-magnification lens to concentrate on certain lunar features. Since you'll be observing in the dark, it's a good idea to learn how to change eyepieces by touch.

ACTIVITY
Changing Eyepieces While Viewing the Moon

You should start your Moon-viewing session with the longest focal-length (lowest-magnification) eyepiece in place. This maximizes the field of view (FOV)—or how much of the sky you can see through the telescope at any one time—and allows you to easily center the Moon in the FOV. With a properly boresighted instrument (see Chapter 2), first center the Moon in the finder scope and then check the image through your telescope's main optics.

You may find that it is necessary to move the tube somewhat until the Moon is exactly centered. Then replace this eyepiece with the next shorter focal-length (or higher-powered) eyepiece, which you pull from your pocket. You should see a brighter and larger Moon image centered in a smaller field of view.

One advantage to practicing on the Moon is that our satellite is bright and easy to locate. This is fortunate because you'll probably "lose" the Moon a few times before you learn how to change eyepieces without moving the telescope. Once you have mastered the art of changing eyepieces without moving the tube, you are ready to "graduate" to viewing planets, stars, or deep-sky objects under increasing magnification.

One very useful (and comparatively inexpensive) accessory for your telescope is a reticle eyepiece. Through such a device, you can view celestial objects together with an illuminated internal scale, which allows you to measure the size of objects as well as determine angular distances between objects. For example, assume that the field of view of your reticle eyepiece is 1 degree of arc, or 1°. If the separation between the two members of a binary star system is ¹⁄₁₀ of your reticle eyepiece's field of view, then these two stars are ¹⁄₁₀ of a degree (or 6 arc minutes) apart.

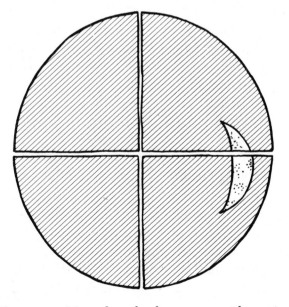

The crescent Moon through a low-power reticle eyepiece

ACTIVITY
Using the Moon to Calibrate a Low-power Reticle Eyepiece

If you attach a low-power reticle eyepiece to your telescope, you can use the internal scale (be it a grid or concentric circles) to estimate the angular extent (size) of planetary features such as the Great Red Spot of Jupiter, Saturn's rings, the Martian polar caps, and various deep-sky objects. You can also use the internal scale to measure the separation of binary stars.

A good way to practice with this handy tool is by finding a lunar feature. With the help of a moon map, first practice viewing the Moon and identifying various features. The full Moon has an average angular extent of slightly more than $1/2$ of a degree. By using the scale to estimate the fraction of the Moon's disc covered by a feature under observation, and counting the number of scale divisions covered by that feature, you can determine the angular separation of the reticle's divisions.

Fun with Filters

A number of optical accessories exist that allow the telescope owner to change the color quality of the light reaching his or her eye. Neutral density (ND) filters, which equally reduce the intensity of all colors, can reduce the intensity of sunlight so that solar features can be viewed safely. Color-selective filters can also be purchased that highlight certain solar or planetary features and that even reduce (within limits) the effects of street lighting.

Neutral density filters are usually characterized by their ND rating. An ND1 filter reduces the incident light by a factor of 10. Similarly, an ND2 filter transmits only 1 percent of the light striking it. For viewing sunspots or other features on the Sun's visible surface, a filter strength of ND4 is recommended. This will reduce the intensity of the sunlight transmitted to the eye by a factor of 10,000. Before using a filter to view the Sun, remember to protect your eyes by checking that the filter is properly attached to your telescope.

Neutral density filters that cover a telescope's aperture are larger than those that attach to the eyepiece. For this reason, the aperture filters are generally more expensive. The budding solar observer would be ill-advised to succumb to temptation and purchase the less-expensive eyepiece filter, however. The concentrated solar energy may cause high temperatures within the tube that may damage your telescope's optics. Eyepiece filters are fine, however, for viewing celestial objects other than the Sun.

While ND filters operate by equally reducing the intensity of all colors of light transmitted through your eye, color-selective filters transmit only certain colors.

ACTIVITY
Experimenting with Crude Color Filters

Crude but effective color filters can be constructed by stretching a piece of colored (but translucent) cellophane over your binocular or telescope eyepiece or aperture. First, observe a distant traffic light with the naked eye. You will observe that the red and green lights seem to be of about equal intensity. If you observe the same traffic light through green cellophane, the green light will seem brighter than the red. What happens when you observe the same traffic light through a piece of red cellophane?

Next, observe the Moon or a bright planet through your telescope or binoculars with and without a crude color filter attached. Notice how certain features appear dimmer or brighter in certain colors.

To some observers, the Moon's polar regions and edges are best observed through a blue filter. Some of the lunar maria (dark areas or "seas") and craters stand out best when observed through a red filter, at least when the Moon is nearly full.

You'll mostly want to use color-selective filters for viewing the Moon and planets. Certain color combinations are particularly useful in improving the contrast of planetary features. For instance, assume that you wish to observe the planet Mercury. This planet is a difficult target because it's close to the Sun and usually obscured in the orange-red skies of dawn or dusk. You can use a blue filter to cut the intensity of the near-Sun skylight and still allow some of the light reflected from the planet through to your eye. Some specific activities using color filters are included in Chapters 4 and 5.

Mounts and Clock Drives

To this point, only the optical components of a telescope have been discussed. Good lenses and mirrors alone do not a telescope make—some consideration must be given to the mechanical aspects of your viewing equipment.

No matter what type of telescope optics you have, the telescope tube will be placed on a mount, which supports the telescope tube while the viewer points it at a celestial object. There are two basic types of mounts.

The most common telescope mount is the alt–az, which stands for "altitude–azimuth." The altitude is a measure of a star's position above the Earth's horizon, and the azimuth refers to the compass position of that star. For a beginning astronomer, the alt–az mount is the simplest to use. To use this mount, simply rotate the telescope tube until it lines up with the compass direction to the celestial object under observation. Then raise or lower the tube until the object comes into view.

After using an alt–az mount for a while, you'll become aware of its basic disadvantage. Although you can easily find a celestial object, you must constantly tinker with your instrument during the observing session; because, as the Earth spins on its axis, the celestial objects constantly move from the telescope's field of view (FOV).

One means of compensating for Earth motion is to use an equatorial mount. This mount is designed so that you can easily follow an object within the telescope's FOV with a minimum of adjustment. To follow a target, you need to move only one axis of an equatorial mount, not two as with the alt–az mount. To assist in finding faint sky objects, setting circles, marked with celestial coordinates (called declination and right ascension), can be attached to an equatorial mount.

Many amateurs equip their equatorial mounts with a clock drive. This electromechanical device allows the telescope to compensate automatically for the Earth's motion during a viewing session. If you want to view the same celestial object for minutes or hours without adjusting your telescope's pointing direction, a clock drive is a good investment.

Finding Your Way in the Sky: Star Wheels, Star Charts, Atlases, and Software

If you visit the gift shop of your local planetarium or science museum, or glance through the pages of an astronomy magazine, you'll find a wide variety of products to help a novice astronomer find objects in the heavens. One of the nicest products is the star wheel, which costs only a few dollars.

Sold at planetariums and science centers, the star wheel adjusts to present the positions of the brightest stars in the sky for any night of the year and any time of night. If you hold your star wheel overhead, as its directions indicate, you'll soon be able to recognize prominent constellations and bright stars. To preserve your night-adapted vision while studying constellations outdoors, you should use a red-tinted flashlight to illuminate the dial of the star wheel. You can make one of these by putting red cellophane around a regular flashlight.

Monthly star charts that show the Moon and planets as well as the bright stars are published in many magazines and newspapers. Some of the best are mailed free four times a year to members of the Astronomical Society of the Pacific (390 Ashton Avenue, San Francisco, CA 94112). These are of great use in planning an evening observing session. Often, star charts discuss special sky events. You may learn about close alignments of two or more planets (called *conjunctions*), eclipses, meteor showers, and other forthcoming sky happenings by regularly reading the star chart in your newspaper.

If you decide to concentrate on dimmer objects, you might wish to purchase a star atlas. Some of these present the few thousand sky objects visible to

With an equatorial mount, this astronomer can easily follow an object as it moves across the sky.

the unaided eye from a dark, rural location. Others present the positions of millions of stars that are visible through binoculars or small telescopes. A good atlas will tell you about observing binary and multiple stars and variable stars that vary in brightness. The location, brightness, and color of deep-sky objects—nebulae and galaxies—are also described.

You can use your star atlas to prepare finder charts that will assist you in locating faint objects through your telescope. A finder chart shows bright and faint objects and star patterns near objects of interest. You use a finder chart as a map. You focus on a bright star and move the telescope tube a few degrees east or north to locate your celestial target.

ACTIVITY
Creating a Finder Card

To perform this activity, you'll need some materials in addition to your telescope. These include a star atlas, index cards, a pen or pencil, a ruler, and a compass to help you draw good circles. You'll also need access to a photocopying machine.

Experienced amateur and professional astronomers often find their way around the sky with pre-prepared star-field maps on index cards. You can prepare these directly from your star atlas for use with your telescope.

Assume that your telescope has a field of view of 6 degrees and you want to survey all stars visible to the naked eye within the field of view when you are centered on a selected bright star (Vega, for example). First, look up Vega on the appropriate chart in your atlas and photocopy the page.

Note that one of the coordinates of stars pictured in your atlas is degrees of arc. Use your ruler to determine how many inches or centimeters correspond to a degree of arc on the atlas page. This is the "scale" of the atlas page.

Then, with the aid of a compass and the scale of the atlas page, draw a circle with a radius of 3 degrees centered on Vega. (Using the enlargement/reduction feature available on many photocopying machines, you can convert your Vega field of view to any comfortable size.) Cut the circle from the photocopied page and paste it to an index card.

When you observe next, bring along the index card and a red-tinted flashlight. With a little practice, soon you will be able to identify all the stars included in your finder card that are in the field of view with Vega.

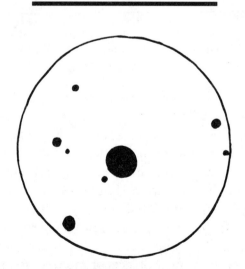

A finder card for bright stars within about 5 degrees of Vega (large central circle). Most telescopes present an inverted image (north on top).

Today, many atlases are computerized. Astronomical software, which is frequently advertised and reviewed in astronomy magazines, is useful to the amateur astronomer who owns a personal computer as well as a telescope. Some of these computerized star atlases can depict significant sky events years in the future. Many of them have beautiful full-color graphics.

Coordinate Systems—Finding Your Way around the Sky

Say that you've discovered a supernova and wish to quickly communicate your discovery to the rest of the astronomical community. You could call the newspaper or television and say, "I've just discovered an exploding star—it's about 15 degrees and 7 minutes west of Vega and 3 degrees and 18 minutes north of that star."

What you are doing is using the bright stars as a frame of reference. Any astronomer who knows a bit about angular measure can point his or her instrument to the right spot in the sky.

The stars do move around, however. Over a period of many thousands or millions of years, the relative positions of Vega and your supernova will change. Because astronomy is such an ancient discipline, one that considers very long time scales, astronomers often use coordinates that are based upon Earth coordinates rather than on other sky objects.

The astronomical system of declination and right ascension is based upon the terrestrial method of latitude and longitude. You know that on Earth the latitude lines circle the globe parallel to the equator. The longitude lines go around the Earth through the poles.

In the sky, we can find a celestial equivalent of latitude by imagining that the Earth's pole projects skyward. *Declination* is the celestial equivalent of latitude and is measured in degrees. Therefore, the North Pole star Polaris is near "declination 90 degrees north," or "declination +90 degrees." If there were a bright South Pole star, its declination would be "90 degrees south" or "−90 degrees."

The celestial equivalent of longitude is called *right ascension*. This is measured eastward in the sky from the position of the Sun on the first day of spring. Units of right ascension are identical to units of time: hours, minutes, and seconds. A separation of 1 hour of right ascension (called an *hour angle*) corresponds to an angular shift east or west of 15 degrees.

Your star atlas will list the celestial coordinates (declination and right ascension) accurate for a particular terrestrial date. The long-term motion of the Earth's poles, which is called *precession,* is corrected for in periodic updates to star coordinates. Because the precession cycle requires 26,000 years, your star atlas will give many lifetimes of accurate service!

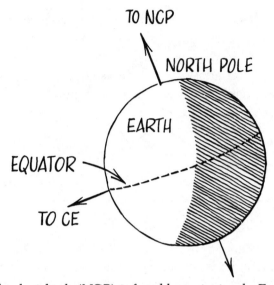

The north celestial pole (NCP) is found by projecting the Earth's North Pole into space. If you are standing at the Earth's equator, the celestial equator (CE) is directly overhead.

PART 2
★ ★ ★

Observing with Your Telescope

★ ★ ★

★4★
Observing the Moon

*T*he first time you use your telescope or binoculars for astronomical view-ing, it will probably be a clear, moonlit night. Take the scope outside and assemble it. To start observing, use your lowest-power eyepiece. On cold or hot nights, wait about half an hour for the temperature of the optics and tube to become equal to that of the surrounding air.

Point the aperture at the Moon and focus the eyepiece. The Moon is the best place to start your skywatch because it's so easy to find. The view is im-pressive. You may go on to view distant planets, stars, and galaxies; but it is your first telescopic image of the Moon, our planet's one natural satellite, that will hook you forever as an amateur astronomer!

Although much smaller than the Earth, the Moon is obviously a world in its own right. Right away, you'll notice the large, flat, dark regions called *maria* (the plural of *mare*—Latin for "sea"), impressive craters, and mountains that rival Mount Everest in height.

Even with a small telescope or a pair of binoculars, you can view many of these features. If you observe for a series of days, you'll see many of the features cast shadows that become long or short as the *terminator* (the line separating dark and sunlit areas on the Moon) shifts during the cycle of lunar phases.

The Moon Close Up

Through your low-power eyepiece, you'll notice immediately that some lunar features are darker than others. In most lunar lighting conditions, the flat, low maria are darker than the surrounding highlands. The different color of various lunar features is caused by differing types of rock.

Craters of all sizes pockmark the Moon's face. The largest of these, which are 100 to 200 kilometers (60 to 120 miles) across and are clearly visible in binoculars or through a low-power telescope lens, give evidence to the Moon's billion-year bombardment by asteroids and comets. Because the Moon has no atmosphere or oceans, the craters do not erode, so they've remained much the same through time. (The Earth has been struck as often as the Moon, but only the most-recent craters—such as Meteor Crater in Arizona—remain.)

Some of the lunar craters have walls several kilometers high. Many of these walls cast shadows on the surrounding plains when the Moon is less than full. Other craters have straight lines coming out of them that look a bit like the spokes of a wagon wheel. These are called *rays*. Rayed craters were formed when the force of asteroidal or cometary impacts projected streams of molten material tens or hundreds of kilometers across the relatively flat lunar plains.

Most of the human and robotic expeditions to the Moon have landed in the flat plains rather than in the more treacherous highlands. Many robotic lunar expeditions have been mounted by the American, Russian, and Japanese space programs, and six 2-person crews of the American Apollo program have touched down on the Moon.

Photo of the Moon showing the terminator, the line dividing day and night (Lick Observatory photograph)

 ACTIVITY
Locating Lunar Landing Sites

You can use the Moon maps on pages 56–57 to help you locate the landing sites of the various lunar expeditions. One way of doing this is to become familiar with the shapes of lunar features near the landing sites, such as crater alignments and the outlines of the maria.

Then, when the Moon is nearly full, go outside with your telescope and try to pick out the same features. You'll find that a low- or medium-power eyepiece will be ample for locating most of the landing sites. Soon you'll be able to point out to your friends where the first expeditions from Earth landed on our nearest celestial neighbor.

1. The first moon-landing expedition, *Apollo 11*, touched down within Mare Tranquilitatis in July 1969. A few months later, the astronauts aboard *Apollo 12* explored Oceanus Procellarum. Can you find these two seas?

2. In 1971, *Apollo 14* returned to the eastern portion of the Moon's visible face, touching down between Oceanus Procellarum and Sinus Medii. Approximately where would this spot be?

3. A few months later, two astronauts aboard the *Apollo 15* mission visited the eastern edge of Mare Serenitatis. Where were they?

_____

When the Moon passes in between the Earth and the Sun, we can observe that awesome, but infrequent, celestial event called the total solar eclipse. During a lunar eclipse, the Earth lines up in between the Moon and the Sun. The Earth blocks some of the light that ordinarily falls on the Moon, thus making the Moon appear darker. Both events can be predicted well in advance by astronomers. You can find out about the dates and locations of future eclipses from newspapers, almanacs, and sky manuals.

The Phases of the Moon

You've probably noticed how the Moon seems to get larger (*waxes*) and smaller (*wanes*) and larger again during a regular cycle. The cycle during which the Moon waxes and wanes is called the *lunar month.*

When the Moon and the Sun are closest together in the sky, the face of the Moon that faces the Earth is dark. This is called the new Moon.

As the Moon revolves around the Earth, it begins to move away from the Sun. More and more of its face is illuminated. The Moon is waxing, or growing bigger.

A sliver of a Moon appears a few days after the new phase. This is called the waxing crescent. About seven days after the new phase, the Moon seems to be half-illuminated. This is the first-quarter Moon.

When the Moon grows larger than its first quarter and appears to be three-quarters illuminated, it is in the waxing gibbous phase (*gibbous* meaning "humpbacked").

Halfway through the lunar cycle and 14 days after the new Moon, the visible face of the Moon is fully illuminated. This is called the full Moon. The Moon then begins to get smaller, or wane. On its way back to the new phase, it passes through the waning gibbous, Third Quarter, and waning crescent phases.

Using a sketch pad, crayons, or pastels, you may want to sketch the appearance of the Moon during its various phases through your telescope. After you go inside, you can use the Moon map from pages 56–57 to label various features.

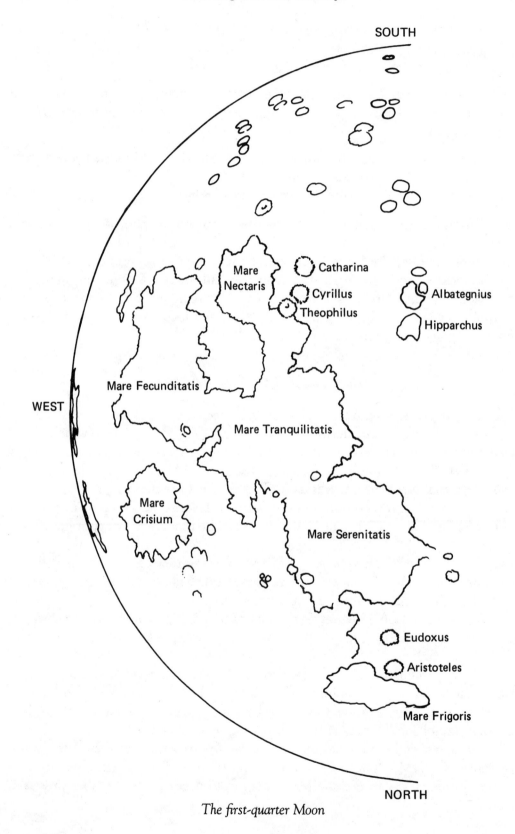

The first-quarter Moon

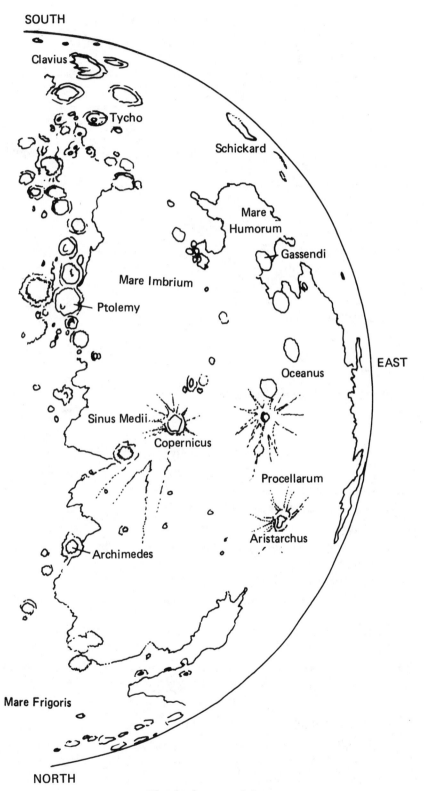

SOUTH

Clavius

Tycho

Schickard

Mare
Humorum

Gassendi

Mare Imbrium

Ptolemy

Sinus Medii

Copernicus

Oceanus

EAST

Procellarum

Aristarchus

Archimedes

Mare Frigoris

NORTH

The third-quarter Moon

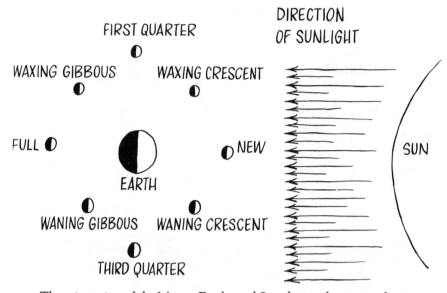

The orientation of the Moon, Earth, and Sun during the various lunar phases (Note: Distances and sizes are not to scale.)

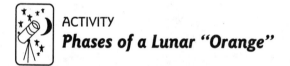

ACTIVITY
Phases of a Lunar "Orange"

To understand the Moon's phases, try this activity in a darkened room with a friend, a flashlight, and a circular object such as an orange. Imagine that the orange is the Moon. Light from the flashlight represents sunlight. Put the orange on a table and ask your friend to illuminate the fruit with the flashlight.

When you stand behind your friend, the orange is completely illuminated, or in the "full phase." If you walk around the table until the orange is exactly between you and the light beam, the orange is completely dark, or "new." Continue walking around the illuminated fruit to observe other orange "phases."

Sometimes, on a clear night from a dark location, you will notice that the dark portion of a crescent Moon or new Moon is slightly visible. This effect is called *Earthshine*, and is caused by the reflection of sunlight from the Earth's atmosphere. Some of this light strikes the Moon and is reflected back toward the observer.

Another beautiful lunar effect can be seen during the full phase when high-altitude temperatures in the Earth's atmosphere are low enough for cirrus (or ice) clouds to form. Moonlight scattered by the high-altitude ice crystals will form one or more halos around the Moon.

The different lunar phases are best observed at different times of day. In its new phase, the Moon rises at sunrise and sets at sunset. Therefore, this phase is not observable.

The waxing crescent Moon rises in the morning and sets in the evening. You can often spot the waxing crescent Moon low in the western sky at sunset.

In the first quarter, the Moon is easily observed during the early evening. During the waxing gibbous phase, the Moon rises in the afternoon and sets before dawn.

The full Moon, which is highest in the sky at midnight, rises at sundown and sets at sunrise. In its waning phases, the Moon becomes a less-desirable observing target, unless you are a night owl.

 ACTIVITY
Observing the First-quarter Moon

The first-quarter Moon rises at noon and sets at midnight. Because the Moon is well above the western horizon at dusk, many amateur astronomers observe it during this phase.

As the Sun is setting, set your telescope up outdoors with a low-power eyepiece in place. Use the finder scope to center the Moon in the eyepiece. The western half of the Moon is fully illuminated during the first-quarter phase.

The *Apollo 11* landing site, Mare Tranquilitatis, is easy to find during this phase. The floors of many craters stand out in sharp relief. Jagged shadows on the lunar surface are cast by crater walls and mountains.

Other lunar seas visible during the first quarter-phase include Mare Fecunditatis, Mare Crisium, Mare Serenitatis, Mare Frigoris, and Mare Nectaris. The large craters Theophilus, Cyrillus, and Catharina are also easily visible. You'll also enjoy viewing the walled plains called Eudoxus, Aristoteles, and Hipparchus.

Finding Lunar Features

A wide variety of features on the Moon can be viewed through binoculars or a small telescope. You will probably find that your most rewarding lunar observing sessions will not be during a full Moon. The full Moon is very bright, making the observation of surface detail more difficult. Also, features near the center of the Moon's visible face will not cast shadows during a full Moon, because the Sun is directly overhead.

The walled craters are a lunar feature that you may find interesting to view at various stages of the lunar cycle. The largest of these, Clavius, is about 240 kilometers (145 miles) across. The walls of this crater tower 3.6 kilometers (2.3 miles) above the surrounding terrain. Clavius is located toward the southern edge of the Moon's visible face. Careful observers will notice that Clavius contains mountains even higher than its walls.

ACTIVITY
Sunrise in Clavius

Because of its high walls and the mountain chains and smaller craters within it, the Clavius crater is wonderful to observe through binoculars or a low-power telescope. When the Moon is past its first quarter, you can observe the sunrise in this crater during the early evening hours. Clavius, as shown in your Moon map, is close to the Moon's south pole (on the top of the inverted image through your telescope).

First, you'll notice bright points of light appearing above a dark background. These are the peaks on the floor of the crater [some of which tower a full kilometer (about 0.6 mile) above the crater walls], glinting in the rays of the rising Sun.

As the Sun climbs higher, details gradually become visible on the floor of Clavius. Finally, the southeastern wall of the giant crater becomes visible. Note how the shadows cast by features within the crater decrease in size as the Sun climbs in the sky.

Between the Moon's eastern rim and the small, dark plain called Sinus Medii is the magnificent walled crater Copernicus, which is ⅓ the diameter of Clavius and also boasts 3.6 kilometer (2.2 mile) walls. Tycho, a southern crater slightly larger than Copernicus, also has 3.6 kilometer (2.2 mile) walls and is a fine example of a rayed crater. At full Moon, Tycho is the most prominent lunar crater. A fascinating observing project is to watch the variation in the length of the shadows cast by these craters' walls as the Moon ages from new to full and back to new.

ACTIVITY
Spotting Smaller Craters Using Higher Magnification

As you shift from low to medium to high magnification, you'll notice that more lunar details become visible through your telescope eyepiece. Using each eyepiece, try counting how many craters are visible on a particular portion of the Moon.

If you carefully sketch the visible craters within a selected portion of the Moon, you may be able to locate (and even name) these craters on a Moon map more detailed than the ones in this chapter. Full-color Moon maps, good for low or medium telescope magnification, are included in D. Baker's *The Henry Holt Guide to Astronomy* (NY: Henry Holt, 1990). More detailed black-and-white Moon maps, which are inverted for easy use with the astronomical telescope, are included in D. H. Menzel and J. M. Pasachoff's *A Field Guide to Stars and Planets*, 2d ed. (Boston, MA: Houghton Mifflin, 1983).

Another fun observing project is to observe which large lunar features are visible at different phases of the lunar cycle. This can be done with binoculars or a low-power telescope eyepiece. If you'd like to sketch the large lunar features visible through your telescope's eyepiece, be sure to use a red-tinted flashlight to illuminate the sketch pad. This protects your dark-adapted vision.

When using your telescope and sketch pad together, you may find it convenient to place the sketch pad on a portable easel or similar mount. Then, after a little practice, you'll be able to watch the Moon through one eye while you check your drawing through the other. Because learning to sketch lunar features may take a while, you'll find an equatorial mount (and perhaps even a clock drive) to be invaluable.

 ACTIVITY
Sketching the March of the Terminator

Begin this project after the new Moon and regularly sketch the Moon's appearance during the next 14 days, as the Moon waxes to the full phase.

New to First Quarter   Just after the new Moon, the western edge of the Moon becomes illuminated. Following the terminator from north to south, you should be able to locate Mare Crisium and Mare Fecunditatis. Long shadows point toward the east, which improves the visibility of lunar features.

As the first-quarter phase approaches, the terminator crosses Mare Nectaris and Mare Tranquilitatis, both landing sites for Apollo missions. As you proceed south along the terminator, the large craters Theophilus, Cyrillus, and Catharina are easy to find. Theophilus has a central mountain and 5.5-kilometer-(3.3-mile) high walls.

Just before the first quarter, the terminator crosses Hipparchus, a striking walled plain with a diameter of 160 kilometers (100 miles). Moving north along the terminator, you come to the eastern edge of Mare Serenitatis, the walled plains Eudoxus and Aristoteles, and finally Mare Frigoris.

First Quarter to Full   While observing in the first-quarter phase, you'll notice that the visible contrast of lunar features starts to decrease. This is because the higher Sun is reducing the length of shadows cast by the lunar features. During the first quarter, the terminator crosses Sinus Medii, a small and dark feature near the center of the lunar disk.

As the Moon approaches the waxing gibbous phase, the terminator crosses the 80-kilometer (50-mile) diameter walled plain Archimedes and then the walled crater Copernicus near the Moon's equator. Shortly before the full Moon, the terminator crosses Mare Humorum in the Moon's southeast quadrant. You may notice that this "sea" is sprinkled with white spots at full Moon. Astronomers believe that these spots might be caused by sunlight bouncing off an ancient lava flow.

Just before the full Moon, the terminator crosses the dark plain Oceanus Procellarum and the crater Aristarchus. This crater is of special interest to astronomers studying the Moon.

At full Moon, you'll observe a complete lack of shadows and a reduced visibility of lunar features. As the Moon ages beyond the full Moon, the terminator reappears on the west side of the Moon's visible face. The shadows reappear—now pointed west—and the visual contrast of surface detail improves. The first objects to disappear from the face of the Moon after the full phase are the western "seas" Mare Crisium and Mare Fecunditatis. These were the first lunar features to become visible after the new phase.

Even with a small telescope, you can perform real lunar research if you have a fairly dark observing location and a set of eyepiece filters. After you become familiar with the major landmarks of the Moon's visible surface, you may wish to regularly observe the crater Aristarchus near the Moon's northeast edge.

 LUNAR FILTER ACTIVITY I
Hunting for Blue Flashes

Astronomers have known for decades that the crater Aristarchus sometimes glows blue and violet during the waxing crescent phase. This occasional glow is an example of a transient lunar phenomena (TLP) and may be due to gas emitted from cavities below the lunar surface. Observations by Apollo astronauts orbiting the Moon revealed that radon gas may sometimes be emitted from the Aristarchus region.

TLP events associated with other lunar features have occasionally been observed. Because TLP emissions are colored blue or violet and the surrounding lunar terrain is generally yellow, brown, or gray, blue or violet eyepiece filters will greatly increase the contrast and visibility of TLP events.

If you try this activity, you'll need a dark viewing location and a great deal of patience. Observers fortunate enough to view a TLP event should write a letter to *Sky & Telescope* or *Astronomy* magazines.

Generally, the lunar surface presents few color variations. In a few lunar regions, however, blue, yellow, and red filters can sometimes prove useful in improving the visual contrast.

 LUNAR FILTER ACTIVITY 2
Using Color Filters

The apparent colors of lunar features will vary with the lunar phase, the condition of the Earth's atmosphere, and the sensitivity of your eyes. Careful observations by many professional and amateur astronomers over the years, however, have revealed that blue, yellow, and red filters can sometimes improve the visual contrast of various lunar features. The best time to observe lunar color variations is during the full phase, when the Moon is high in the sky.

Try observing the Moon with your blue filter, for instance. You may find that crater rays and features near the Moon's edge stand out more in blue than in unfiltered light.

Now try observing the Moon through a red filter. Most of the maria will seem even darker through a red filter than through unfiltered light.

Finally, replace your red eyepiece filter with a yellow filter. Lunar crater walls and mountains often appear the brightest in yellow.

After the Sun, the Moon is the brightest object in the sky. At full Moon, you may even notice shadows cast on the Earth by moonlight. Therefore, near full Moon, unfiltered lunar observations through your telescope may be uncomfortable.

Much of the lunar glare can be compensated for by using a neutral density (ND) eyepiece filter specially designed to reduce the intensity of moonlight without changing the color. Thus, you can visually compare the brightness of various lunar features, even when the Moon is full.

ACTIVITY
Comparing the Apparent Brightness of Lunar Features

During different phases, the apparent brightness of lunar features will vary. For instance, mountain ranges and crater walls will be easier to observe when the Moon is less than full, because of the longer shadows. Through an ND filter or in unfiltered light, maria and crater interiors are generally dark. Crater walls and mountains are brighter.

During the 1930s, astronomers developed a 10-point brightness scale. This allows different observers to communicate their impressions of variations in lunar brightness.

On this scale, a brightness of "0" is assigned to shadows on the Moon; a brightness of "10" is assigned to the brightest visual features. The brightness ratings of some prominent features presented on the Moon maps in this chapter are as follows:

Brightness 0   —shadows on the Moon

3.5—inner surface of crater Archimedes

4   —inner surface of Ptolemy

4.5—Sinus Medii

5   —terrain near crater Archimedes

5.5—rays extending from crater Copernicus

8   —walls of crater Copernicus

9.5—inner part of crater Aristarchus

10—central peak of crater Aristarchus

Compare these values with some of the other features you have found on the Moon. How bright would you say these features are: Mare Crisium, Mare Tranquilitatis, crater Tycho, and Oceanus Procellarum?

ACTIVITY
Measuring the Length of a Lunar Feature Using a Reticle Eyepiece

You can use a low-power reticle eyepiece to gauge fairly accurately the extent of a lunar shadow, mare, crater, or other feature, if that feature is close to the center of the Moon's visible face. First, you need to know that the diameter of the Moon is about 3,400 kilometers (2,100 miles).

Next, use the gradations or scale of the reticle eyepiece to compare the sizes of the Moon and the feature of interest. For instance, if the dimension of a particular mare is ⅕ the size of the Moon's diameter, then the mare has a dimension of 3,400/5 or about 700 kilometers (2,100/5 or about 400 miles).

 ACTIVITY
Monitoring the Color of the Eclipsed Moon

If you have a series of color eyepiece filters, you can monitor the condition of the Earth's atmosphere by observing the eclipsed full Moon through each filter. Almanacs and monthly astronomical publications announce in advance where and when a lunar eclipse will occur.

According to the Danjon scale, there are five classifications of lunar eclipses; all of these are based upon lunar color and visibility:

Class 0—very dark, nearly invisible Moon during totality.

Class 1—dark eclipse; gray/brown coloring; lunar details hard to distinguish.

Class 2—dark red/rust coloring; center of Moon darker than edge.

Class 3—brick red central portion of eclipse; brighter (often yellow) border.

Class 4—copper or orange/red central portion of very bright eclipse; bright blue border.

The clearest Earth atmosphere should produce a Class 3 or 4 eclipse. Fog and atmospheric pollution will result in a darker eclipse. Widespread dust in the Earth's upper atmosphere produces the darkest lunar eclipses.

Excellent lunar-eclipse results can be obtained with telescope apertures as low as 5 centimeters (2 inches) and magnifications of 30X–100X. Because lunar eclipses often last for many minutes (in some cases over an hour), you may want to observe continuously during the eclipse and correlate your observations with time. One national organization that might be interested in your eclipse observations is the American Association of Lunar and Planetary Observers in San Francisco, California.

★ 5 ★
Tracking the Planets

About five billion years ago, the Sun did not yet exist. In place of our star and all the planets of the solar system was a vast cloud of dust and gas called a *nebula.*

Initially, this primeval nebula was trillions of kilometers across. Gradually, over millions of years, it contracted. Gravity caused clumps of matter to condense in the swirling gases of the contracting nebula. The clumps became more massive as material condensed around them. As the clumps became more massive, they grew faster and faster.

 ACTIVITY
An "Infant Solar System" in a Pan

At home, you can duplicate some of the conditions in the infant solar system. Place a bit of water in a shallow pan. Add a few spoonfulls of flour. Then stir the mixture at a constant motion in one direction. You'll notice that some clumps form in the mixture as you stir it.

Now add some more flour and mix again. You'll observe that some of the clumps are larger.

What happens as you stir longer—does the mixture become more uniform, or do the clumps thicken? What happens if you speed up or slow down your stirring?

By experimenting with your infant solar system, you can see the types of solar systems that might have formed around other stars. Some might have all their material in one giant planet, called a *black dwarf.* Others might have very small planets, with the largest bodies being comets or asteroids.

As the nebula contracted, it began to flatten out and take on a disklike appearance. At the center of the disk was the large clump that would someday become the Sun. As more material fell into this "protosun," the density, pressure, and temperature near the center of the young star increased. Circling the protosun were many smaller clumps. Over the years, after many mergers and collisions, these became the familiar planets of our solar system.

As the new planets became larger, they acted like giant vacuum cleaners. More and more of the material between them was attracted by their gravitational fields. Dust and gas cleared away between the infant worlds. Trillions of celestial icebergs—young comets containing frozen methane, ammonia, and water—crisscrossed the new solar system.

Eventually, the mass of material forming our star became sufficient for *thermonuclear fusion*—the nuclear reaction that converts hydrogen into helium and energy—to begin.

The Sun turned on! Light and hot gases—the so-called solar wind—began to stream out from the infant star and wash against the largely hydrogen/helium atmospheres of the inner planets. About 4,600 million years ago, the history of the planets had begun.

In this chapter, we'll observe each planet, from the closest to the farthest from the Sun, and discover the fascinating characteristics of each of our neighbors.

The Inner Planets

The closest four planets to the Sun—Mercury, Venus, Earth, and Mars—are the inner planets. These worlds are small and rocky, with comparatively thin atmospheres and few or no natural satellites. For this reason, they are also known as *terrestrial planets.*

Mercury

At about 58 million kilometers (35 million miles) away, Mercury is the closest planet to the Sun. It can also be said that Mercury orbits the Sun at 39 percent of the distance of the Earth from the Sun. The average Earth–Sun separation of about 150 million kilometers (93 million miles) is often referred to as 1 *astronomical unit,* or 1 AU. Therefore, Mercury is 0.39 AU from the Sun.

The intense sunlight and solar wind at Mercury's orbit are too extreme for that small world to possess an atmosphere. In many ways, Mercury resembles the Moon.

 ACTIVITY
Observing Mercury

Like Venus, Mars, Jupiter, and Saturn, Mercury was known to pretelescopic astronomers. Therefore, it is classified as a naked-eye planet.

Observing this small world is quite challenging because it is so close to the Sun and because our sky is more polluted than it was in ancient times. This author has seen Mercury only once—and that was just after dusk through the pristine skies of rural New England.

If you live in or can visit a rural, unpolluted site, you might want to try finding this small world. The monthly magazines *Sky & Telescope* and *Astronomy* list the best times to observe Mercury. These occur when this planet is farthest from the Sun, as viewed from the Earth. You may be able to catch a glimpse of tiny Mercury just after sunset or just before dawn.

Under the best observing conditions, a telescope aperture of 7.5–10 centimeters (3–4 inches) will reveal that Mercury has phases. The time from one "full Mercury" to the next is 116 days.

Venus

Venus, at 0.72 AU from the Sun, is in some ways a twin of the Earth. On an imaginary scale, Venus would weigh in at about 82 percent of one Earth-weight. Venus is also very close in physical size to the Earth.

But that's where the resemblance between the two worlds ends. It seems that after the inner planets lost their original atmospheres, they gained new atmospheres through cometary bombardment and volcanic eruption. On the Earth, the early stages of the atmosphere-building process were similar to those of Venus. However, because Earth is farther from the Sun—and therefore exposed to less sunlight—temperatures built up more slowly on Earth than on our neighbor world.

Today, 4,500 million years after its formation, the surface of Venus is a hellish place. The pressure of Venus's atmosphere is about 95 times the Earth's surface level atmospheric pressure. Typical Venusian surface temperatures are hot enough to melt lead! If that's not enough to discourage Venus-bound astronauts, the atmosphere of this planet is mostly poisonous carbon dioxide, with a trace of corrosive sulfric acid. Even the sturdiest Earth robots that have landed on Venus during the past few decades have survived for only a few hours.

 ACTIVITY
Observing Venus

Because Venus is an inferior planet (meaning that it's closer to the Sun than the Earth is), it experiences a cycle of phases. This cycle repeats every 584 days. Although you won't see much surface detail through the planet's dense atmosphere, Venus is a beautiful sight when viewed at low to moderate power.

Look for it shortly after sunset in the western sky or just before dawn in the east. Blue eyepiece filters are superior to red and yellow filters for observing Venus, because variations in the planet's cloudy atmosphere stand out more in blue. Since this planet is always fairly close to the Sun in the sky, be careful not to point your instrument at the Sun when focusing on Venus!

Venus cannot be observed at its full phase because then it's on the other side of the Sun from the Earth. It is brightest when in the crescent phase. Because of its dense cloud bank, Venus will always be a bright object through your telescope—sometimes the brightest sky object after the Sun and Moon.

Mars

When people think about space travel, their attention naturally turns to Mars, the Red Planet. Weighing in at only $\frac{1}{10}$ of an Earth-weight on our imaginary scale, Mars is much smaller than our world.

Your weight on Mars would be about 60 percent less than your weight on Earth. A Martian day is almost identical in length to an Earth day. However, a year on Mars is almost twice as long. Mars has two small moons, Deimos and Phobos, which are each only about 20 kilometers (12 miles) wide.

Mars's atmosphere is very thin and still evolving. Mars is a cold, dry place at the surface. Although some water ice can be seen in the planet's polar ice caps, much more water must be trapped in a permanent subsurface ice layer. Temperatures at the polar caps of Mars are so low that much of the frozen material there is solid carbon dioxide—a substance commonly called *dry ice*. Dry ice forms when carbon dioxide freezes—at about $-57°C$ ($-70°F$).

Many American and Russian robot space probes have visited this mysterious world. Some have simply flown by Mars, others have orbited the planet or landed there. We know that the planet's predominant red color is due to a combination of water and iron oxide. On Earth, this combination is called *rust*.

A large number of fascinating Martian landforms have been photographed—huge crater fields, a rift valley that dwarfs the Grand Canyon, and number of enormous volcanic mountains. Some of these volcanoes, which may erupt at intervals of millions of years, are much larger than the highest of Earth's mountains.

There are seasonal changes on Mars that can be viewed from Earth, as well as from orbiting spacecraft, using small telescopes. It is now known that some of these changes are due to widespread, even planetwide, dust storms.

Intelligent Martians?

Because of the polar caps and seasonal changes, astronomers have speculated for years about the possibility of life on Mars. In 1877, the Italian astronomer Giovanni Schiaparelli first reported the existence of a network of straight lines on Mars that came to be called canals. A century ago, many people believed that these Martian canals were a vast irrigation system designed to transport water from the planet's poles to an ancient civilization that was thought to have thrived near the planet's equator. It is now known, however, that all or most of the canals are optical illusions caused by the eye's connecting craters and other features at the limit of visibility.

For decades, authors wrote about fictional Martians, astronomers sought to map the canals, and people speculated about communicating with or visiting these interplanetary neighbors. When a radio version of H. G. Wells's classic *War of the Worlds* was broadcast as a 1938 Halloween prank, thousands of listeners believed that a Martian invasion was in progress and panicked.

Since *Mariner IV* flew by Mars in 1964, many robot spacecraft have visited that planet. Although signs of existing intelligent (or lower) Martian life-forms have not been found, some astronomers speculate that Mars may have been an abode of life in the distant past.

In the early decades of the twenty-first century, manned spaceships may be sent to visit the Red Planet. The astronauts aboard these first ships from Earth to Mars will hope to learn conclusively whether the Red Planet has ever harbored life. Perhaps within your lifetime, astronauts will be living on Mars in domed cities resembling sealed greenhouses. Who knows, the Martian environment could be gradually modified to become more Earthlike (a process called *terraforming*).

ACTIVITIES
Observing Mars

Mars comes closest to the Earth at intervals of a little over two years. At that time, the two planets are separated by as little as 56 million kilometers (35 million miles).

High in the sky, within the constellations of the zodiac and easily found with the unassisted eye, Mars is a fascinating object to observe through a telescope. With a telescope aperture of 10–15 centimeters (4–6 inches), you can keep track of Martian seasonal changes and observe many of the larger surface features. Good accessories for Mars observers include a set of eyepiece filters and a reticle eyepiece.

Rewarding observation of Mars does require some patience. You may have to

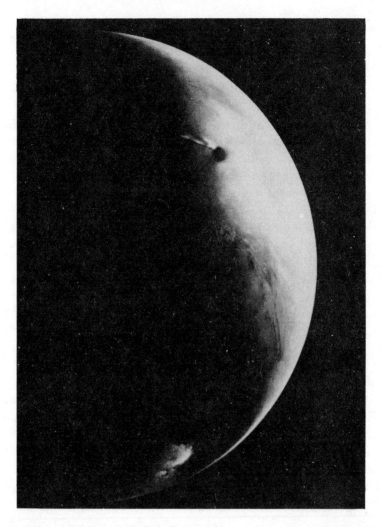

The Viking 2 orbiter took this photo of dawn on Mars in 1977. Visible just to the right of the terminator is the Martian volcano Ascreus Mons, with bright water ice clouds to its left. (Courtesy NASA)

observe for some time before the atmospheres of the Earth and Mars are calm enough for you to obtain good views of the Martian surface.

But even with a small telescope, your patience will be rewarded. You will be able to observe the Martian polar caps as they wax and wane with the seasons, atmospheric phenomena, and the vast red deserts of that planet.

Good color filters will greatly enhance your experience of the Red Planet. A yellow filter is of some use in enhancing the contrast of the Martian polar caps and white clouds (which are possibly low-level ice clouds or mists). But orange and red filters are superior for viewing Martian polar caps and white clouds.

Fine detail on the Martian plains is easier to spot with an orange filter, because it

In 1979, Viking Lander 2 transmitted this image of a thin layer of water ice on the rocks and soil of Mars from its Utopia Planitia landing site. (Courtesy NASA)

will reduce the intensity of the plains' prevailing reddish hue. The darker Martian areas, or maria, will also show better contrast when viewed through an orange filter.

If you are observing at low powers and under steady seeing conditions, a red filter might be superior to an orange. The color contrast between the dark maria and red Martian plains is somewhat more evident in red light.

A green filter is useful in monitoring seasonal changes to the Martian polar caps. It helps you to see better the boundary between the frozen polar cap material (water ice and frozen carbon dioxide) and the surrounding terrain. Green filters also help in observing the yellow clouds that are the precursors of planetwide dust storms on Mars.

Through a blue filter, you may be able to detect water clouds high above Martian surface.

The Outer Planets

The farthest five planets from the Sun—Jupiter, Saturn, Uranus, Neptune, and Pluto—are the outer planets. With the exception of distant, tiny Pluto (which may be an escaped satellite of Neptune or an enormous comet), these outer worlds are large and massive, and they have thick atmospheres and many satellites. They are called the *Jovian planets,* or *gas giants.*

Although only Saturn has a ring system that can be seen through your telescope, it is known from information transmitted by robot spacecraft that the other gas giants (Jupiter, Uranus, and Neptune) also have rings. Planetary rings are made up of dust and ices of material like ammonia, methane, and water.

The main difference between the inner and outer planets is the greater intensity of sunlight that reaches the planets closer to the Sun and the solar wind in the inner solar system. In the inner solar system, the heat of the sun and the solar wind are so intense that the early atmospheres of the planets were evaporated or modified. Beyond Mars, the planets are probably much like they were in the early days of the solar system.

Jupiter

Jupiter, truly the "king of the planets," has a diameter of more than 11 times that of the Earth. Jupiter would tip our imaginary scale at almost 318 Earth-weights. Although the Sun is 1,000 times heavier still, Jupiter can be thought of as a star that failed. If it were a few times larger, thermonuclear reactions would have ignited near Jupiter's core. There would then be two Suns in our sky!

Jupiter is also considerably larger than our planet. More than 1,000 Earths could comfortably fit within Jupiter's enormous volume. (However, more than a million Earths could fit within the Sun!)

Jupiter has at least 16 natural satellites. Most of these are far too small to be observed from the Earth. But four of them—Callisto, Europa, Ganymede, and Io—are large enough to be observed through a small telescope or binoculars. These satellites, first discovered by Galileo with his early refracting telescope, are worlds in their own right. All except for Europa are larger than the Earth's Moon. In fact, Ganymede is a bit larger, and Callisto a little smaller, than the planet Mercury.

 ACTIVITY
Observing Jupiter—Hunting for the Satellites

The four large satellites of Jupiter are so bright that three of them would be visible to the unassisted eye if they were not lost in the glare of the much brighter giant planet. You can easily observe them through your low-power eyepiece or finder scope.

As you observe Jupiter through the telescope, note that as many as four bright starlike objects are arranged in a straight line extending from the planet's equator. These are the satellites (in order of decreasing brightness) Ganymede, Io, Europa, and Callisto. Of these four satellites, Io is the closest to Jupiter and Callisto is the farthest. Although space probes have revealed that they are worlds in their own right, these satellites are too distant and small for your telescope to resolve detail on their surfaces.

If a satellite is missing, it is passing either in front of (*transiting*) or behind Jupiter.

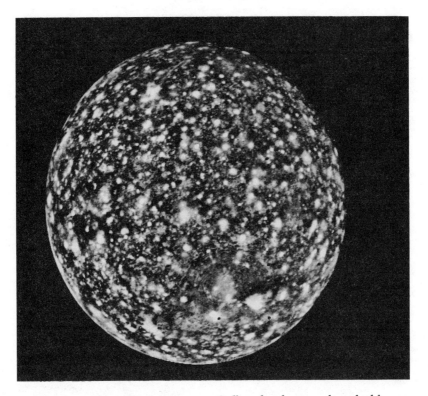

The icy surface of Jupiter's moon Callisto has been pockmarked by asteroids and comets for billions of years. (Courtesy NASA)

If one of the large satellites is transiting Jupiter, you may (under higher magnification) be able to observe the shadow of that satellite on the planet's cloud banks. Check the pages of *Sky & Telescope* or *Astronomy* magazines for regular updates on Jupiter's large moons.

The American robot spacecraft *Pioneer 10* and *11* and *Voyager 1* and *2* flew past Jupiter on their way out of the solar system. Many photos of Jupiter's satellites, rings, and colorful cloud bands were returned to Earth.

Largely as a result of these expeditions, a great deal more is known about the large moons of Jupiter. Callisto, the most distant of the large satellites from Jupiter, is pockmarked with craters. Its surface seems to be a combination of rock and ice. Ganymede, the largest satellite in our solar system, has cratered and grooved regions. There may be more ice than rock in this satellite's crust. Ganymede is relatively flat—no mountains higher than about 1 kilometer (0.6 mile) exist there.

Europa displays a banded surface that is thought to be the result of cracks in the frozen crust of a Europa-wide ocean. At least in some locations, the European ocean may be warmed by subsurface heat sources.

No, these are not the long-lost canals of Mars! This photo shows cracks in the frozen crust of Europa, one of Jupiter's moons. (Courtesy NASA)

Io is so close to Jupiter (about 400,000 kilometers, or 240,000 miles) that the giant world causes internal stresses within its satellite. This satellite has a thin atmosphere of sulfur dioxide that is fed by many active volcanoes on the satellite's surface.

 ACTIVITIES
Observing Jupiter

A small telescope reveals that Jupiter's atmosphere is divided into alternating horizontal (latitudinal) dark-and-light-colored strips or bands. On a clear night, the atmosphere of Jupiter will be quite colorful to the telescopic observer. One of the most colorful and easy to find features in the Jovian atmosphere is the Great Red Spot, a disturbance that was first observed in 1630 and is easily big enough to swallow the Earth!

Everyone who has viewed the largest planet in our solar system through the telescope has marveled at the colorful "surface" of Jupiter. More sophisticated observers realize that these red-orange-brown-white color patterns are in the planet's dense, thick atmosphere. It is far from clear, in fact, whether a solid surface actually exists beneath these dense clouds.

Although you can see the multicolored Jovian cloud bands without eyepiece filters, a number of color filters can improve the contrast of various features in the Jovian atmosphere. A medium-blue filter will make the Great Red Spot, as well as the horizontal belts closet to Jupiter's equator, stand out. Various other atmospheric features, including those that look like ovals and white spots, will also stand out in the blue.

Try using an orange filter when observing some of the horizontal belts, detail in the equatorial zone of the planet, and white spots. Perhaps the best filter for observing Jupiter is a green-bandpass filter. Viewed in the green spectral range, the contrast of the belts, the Great Red Spot, smaller spots, and white ovals is enhanced.

Saturn

Beyond Jupiter, at an average distance of 9.5 AU from the Sun, is the beautiful world called Saturn. Physically a bit smaller than Jupiter, Saturn would weigh as much as 95 Earth-weights on our imaginary scale. More than 830 Earths could fit within the planet Saturn.

The cloud bands of Saturn are less colorful than those of Jupiter. Like Jupiter, Saturn is attended by many natural satellites. Titan, the largest of these, is larger than the planet Mercury and has a nitrogen and methane atmosphere.

Through a telescope aperture of only 5 centimeters (2 inches), you may be able to catch a glimpse of Titan. With a telescope aperture of 7.5 centimeters (3 inches), Titan will be much clearer, and you'll also notice a 5,000-kilometer (3,000-mile) gap in Saturn's rings called Cassini's Division.

Although Titan is an exciting find through the telescope, you'll probably want to concentrate on observing the magnificent ring system of Saturn. The innermost ring starts 10,000 kilometers (6,000 miles) from Saturn's visible surface (the cloud tops). The outermost ring extends 80,000 kilometers (50,000 miles) from the planet's cloud tops. The rings are very thin, however. The *Pioneer* and *Voyager* probes revealed that these rings are, at their thickest, only a few kilometers thick.

The rings seem to be made up mostly of little pieces of ice and dust. The rings of Saturn (and the less impressive rings of the other giant planets) may be the remains of icy moonlets or comets that approached the planet too closely.

Note the detail in Saturn's ring system. You can also see the shadow of rings on Saturn, as well as the shadow of Saturn on the rings. (Courtesy NASA)

 ACTIVITY
Observing Saturn's Rings

Because of the orbital orientations of the Earth and Saturn, the visual appearance of the rings changes as Saturn orbits the Sun. At intervals of about 15 years, the thin rings actually seem to disappear when viewed edge on. At other times, Saturn with its rings seems like a giant plate viewed from almost directly above.

The rings of Saturn seemed invisible to observers viewing through small telescopes in 1978–1980 and will disappear again in 1995–1996. The rings were at their largest in 1987 and will once again be at their largest in 2003.

An interesting activity for the telescopic observer is to regularly sketch the visual appearance of Saturn's beautiful rings. You can then keep track of the varying aspect of these rings as they periodically appear to disappear or to be at their largest.

With a sufficiently large telescope aperture, you'll be able to see dark divisions between alternate rings. You may also spot bright spots or "ripples" within the rings.

ACTIVITY
Observing Saturn — Viewing Titan

During the times when Saturn's rings are edge on and invisible, the planet will seem to be a bit dimmer. Those are the best times to hunt for Saturn's largest satellite, Titan. The monthly astronomy magazines will let you know when Titan is most visible.

Although invisible to the naked eye, Titan will be easily visible as a starlike object through a 7.5-centimeter (3-inch) aperture telescope. Check the pages of *Sky & Telescope* and *Astronomy* magazines to learn when Titan is passing behind or in front of Saturn, so that you can avoid these times in your Titan search.

Observations of Saturn and its beautiful ring system are enhanced by color eyepiece filters. Through the filters, you may be able to keep track of changes in the rings or cloud bands of Saturn.

ACTIVITY
Observing Saturn — The Use of Eyepiece Filters

Occasional white spots in the rings can be monitored best through a yellow filter. If you observe such temporary features regularly, you can learn a lot about how Saturn's rings rotate.

At times, certain colors in one curve of the ring system (upper or lower) may seem brighter than in the other curve. You can monitor this effect (which might be due to physical changes within the rings or the Earth's atmosphere) by using a series of optical filters. With your violet filter in place, focus upon Saturn's rings and try to determine whether the upper or lower part of the rings is brighter. Then repeat for blue, green, yellow, orange, and red filters.

As Saturn moves across the sky, repeat your filter observations. If the difference in brightness between the upper and lower parts of the rings changes as Saturn moves across the sky, this effect is probably due to the Earth's atmosphere.

The Telescopic Planets

Beyond Saturn, we come to the realm of the *telescopic planets*, those worlds that were discovered after the invention of the astronomical telescope. Uranus and Neptune are gas giant worlds much smaller than Jupiter and Saturn, but still many times larger than our Earth. On the rim of the solar system is mysterious Pluto and its giant satellite Charon. Pluto, which is considerably smaller than our Moon, may be an escaped satellite of Neptune or an icy refugee from the belt of billions of comets that normally reside much farther out from the Sun.

ACTIVITY
Observing Uranus and Neptune

Uranus, when it is closest to the Sun, is just visible to the unassisted eye under ideal conditions. You may be able to spot this distant world through your low-power telescope eyepiece or even good binoculars. Consult the monthly astronomy magazines about the best times to observe this planet and where to look.

With a magnification of 100X, Uranus will appear to be a yellow-green disk. Through a telescope aperture of 20 centimeters (8 inches), you may be able to see some detail in the planet's clouds.

More distant from the Sun, Neptune is always invisible to the unassisted eye. A magnification of at least 300X is necessary to reveal this planet's greenish disk.

Observing Uranus and Neptune is challenging, even to the experienced sky observer. Even under the best of conditions, one of these distant gas giants will never seem larger than a small green disk, unless you have access to a very large telescope.

Pluto is impossible to observe except through very large, observatory-grade telescopes.

ACTIVITIES
Reticle Eyepiece Observations of the Planets

You'll find that a reticle eyepiece is a particularly nice accessory for viewing planetary features. On Venus, a reticle eyepiece will help you confirm the fact that Venus in the crescent phase is closer to the Earth than in the half or gibbous phase. You can do this by drawing a picture of the planet and recording its apparent size at intervals of a few weeks. (The apparent size of Venus in different phases can be measured by comparing it to the illuminated scale of the reticle eyepiece.)

On Mars, you can keep track of Martian seasonal changes by comparing the angular sizes of the polar caps to the disk of the planet. A reticle eyepiece can also be used to keep track of the growth of planetwide dust storms, as these meterological events (which occur when Mars is closest to the Sun) gradually obscure detail on the planet's surface.

On Jupiter, you might wish to try your hand at regular observations of the oval-shaped Great Red Spot. Located at the top–middle of an inverted astronomical view of this distant world, the Great Red Spot typically has dimensions of 40,000 by 15,000 kilometers (25,000 by 9,000 miles). The color, shape, and location of this turbulent feature are not constant.

One of the most satisfying activities with a reticle eyepiece is the observation of Saturn's rings. Try measuring the apparent size of the rings, as compared with the planet, as the ring aspect changes over the years. Careful observers may note that the rings are partially transparent and that they cast a shadow on the giant planet.

As you will see through your telescope (though not nearly this close up!),
the appearance of Jupiter's Great Red Spot changes from day to day.
(Courtesy NASA)

★ 6 ★
Following the Stars

Beyond the familiar and comforting realm of the planets is a vast and alien space. From the earliest times, humans have tried to make the lonely interstellar spaces and the tremendous number of stars in the sky somehow understandable. One of the first approaches to taming this stellar wilderness was the idea of the constellation. Today, 88 of these commonly accepted patterns of stars are recognized.

Constellations and Asterisms

Most of the accepted constellations in the Northern Hemisphere sky were first named by the ancient peoples of Egypt and Mesopotamia. Some star patterns were named because a star grouping happened to resemble a familiar or fabled animal, such as Leo the Lion, the Great Bear and the Little Bear (also called the Big Dipper and the Little Dipper), Scorpius the Scorpion, and Draco the Dragon. Other constellations were named because of a chance resemblance to some familiar tool or device, such as Lyra the Harp. Finally, some star patterns were named after legendary or real people, such as Orion the Hunter, Hercules the Hero, Gemini the Twins, Andromeda the Princess, and her parents Cepheus the King and Cassiopeia the Queen.

More recent astronomers have invented a variety of star patterns that can help the novice observer find his or her way through the complexity of the night sky. These star patterns are called *asterisms*.

The constellation Orion

ACTIVITY
Finding Constellations and Asterisms

Before trying to find star patterns in the sky, you may want to try to recognize them on the seasonal sky charts in this chapter. The Big Dipper and the Little Dipper are the easiest to find. Nor is it difficult to find Orion in the winter/spring sky—the three stars in a row near the center of this constellation clearly resemble a person's belt.

Now look at the chart of the summer sky (p. 94). The three stars of the Summer Triangle, Vega, Deneb, and Altair, are among the brightest sky objects.

Once you learn to recognize a few stars in the sky, you can use them as convenient guideposts during an observing session. Some astronomers make up their own star patterns to help them find other objects in the sky. That's ok—use whatever patterns work for you!

The most familiar asterism to Southern Hemisphere observers is the Southern Cross, which contains the star nearest to our Sun, Alpha Centauri. Prominent in the Northern Hemisphere sky is the asterism called the Summer Triangle. This contains Altair (the brightest star in Aquila the Eagle), Deneb (the brightest star in Cygnus the Swan), and Vega (the brightest star in Lyra the Harp).

To become familiar with the night sky, first look at an obvious sky pattern, such as the Big Dipper. Because it is fairly close to the north celestial pole (an imaginary projection of Earth's North Pole into space), the Big Dipper neither rises nor sets. When viewed from a mid-Northern-Hemisphere location (such as the United States), the Big Dipper is always in the sky. It is therefore called a *circumpolar constellation*.

ACTIVITY
How to Use a Star Atlas

As you become familiar with the bright star patterns in the night sky, you can use these constellations to locate dimmer sky objects. A very handy tool for planning your star observing sessions is a star atlas.

First, you should use a star chart or star wheel set for the season and time of night. Note the location of the brighter stars in the visible constellations and the patterns they make in the sky.

The brightest stars that we can see with the unaided eye are classified as apparent magnitude 0 stars. The dimmest have a magnitude of 1.

Now go to your atlas. Look up a visible constellation in the atlas index, and find the appropriate star map(s) in the atlas for that constellation. The bigger circles on the star map represent the brighter stars, which you can easily find with your naked eye.

Tables for each star map will tell you what interesting objects are in the sky for you to observe through your telescope. After locating a few of these on the star map, try to find them in the sky using the bright stars as landmarks. After a little practice, you'll be able to use your telescope to scan a region of sky between two bright stars in a particular constellation and quickly locate a sky object of interest.

What Are Stars?

In many ways, each of the billions and billions of stars in our universe is a distinct individual. However, like people, stars have certain similarities.

Every star within our galaxy, and more distant galaxies scattered across the universe, initially emerged from one of the dusty "galactic nurseries." As described in the previous chapter, a star contracts for millions of years until temperatures and pressures near the core are high enough to sustain thermonuclear fusion.

Then, the star begins to shine as a stable hydrogen burner, converting hydrogen into helium and energy near its core. Our Sun has been a stable hydrogen burner for almost 5 billion years. It has enough hydrogen fuel to remain in this stage for another 5 billion years or so. Stable, hydrogen-burning stars are also called *main sequence stars*.

In the far future, when the Sun exhausts much of its hydrogen fuel, it will become unstable. The Sun will then expand and cool to become a giant star. Mercury, Venus, and possibly the Earth will vanish into the expanding Sun.

After another 50–100 million years, the giant Sun will have exhausted its remaining fusion fuel and will begin again to contract. After passing through an unstable phase of explosive pulsations, the Sun will end its existence as a white dwarf.

As a white dwarf, the Sun will become hotter and bluer and shine dimly for perhaps a trillion years. At this far-future stage of its development, its physical size will be comparable with that of the Earth. This compact Sun will shine by friction as outer layers collapse gradually toward the core.

All stars go through a similar evolutionary process, but every star doesn't evolve as calmly as our Sun. Hotter, more luminous stars are heavier and bluer than Sunlike stars. These hot, blue stars evolve more rapidly than their cooler cousins. The duration of the stable, hydrogen-burning stage for some of these massive stars may be only a few million years.

After the hydrogen-burning and giant phases, these hot stars undergo a fiery evolution. Instead of pulsating and shrinking gradually toward the white dwarf phase, many of these hot, blue stars become supernova—an enormous

Star-Woman

The late nineteenth and early twentieth centuries were an exciting time in the history of astronomy. Many observatories had large telescopes that were equipped with spectroscopes and cameras. Photographic records of the spectra of millions of stars were being produced; and, because each gas has a different spectra, the spectra revealed what each star was made of.

In order to make sense of all this and learn something about the lives and composition of the stars, someone was needed to patiently evaluate this enormous amount of data. Thus, the stage was set for the champion spectral classifier of all times—Annie Jump Cannon.

Born in 1863, Annie Cannon's early interest in astronomy was sparked by her mother, who was an amateur astronomer. She went on to learn about stellar spectroscopy as an undergraduate at Wellesley College. In 1896, she joined the staff of Harvard College Observatory.

Between 1896 and her death in 1941, Annie Jump Cannon personally analyzed the spectra of more than 500,000 stars! She helped develop the modern scheme that classifies stars according to absolute magnitude, color, and surface temperature.

During her long career, Cannon received many honors, awards, and honorary degrees. In 1938, she was appointed professor of astronomy at Harvard.

Many other women have contributed to the progress of astronomy during the twentieth century. Some, like Annie Cannon, have analyzed stellar spectra. Others have worked as observers or observatory directors or, more recently, have flown in space. All have been inspired by the dedication and scholarship of Annie Jump Cannon, a superheroine of astronomy who clearly deserves the title "Star-Woman."

explosion in which a sizeable fraction of a star's material is almost instantly converted into energy. For a few weeks or months, as the dying star ejects a cloud of gaseous debris, it may outshine all the billions of stars in its galaxy put together.

After the explosion, the star contracts within the surrounding debris. It may become a *neutron star*—a compact object as heavy as the Sun but only 15–20 kilometers (10–12 miles) across. Some neutron stars emit complex patterns of radio waves and are called *pulsars*.

Some initially very heavy stars evolve beyond the neutron star stage, however. These stars can shrink to become so tiny that they are able to alter the fabric of the universe around them. Called *black holes*, these tiny, dense objects act as celestial vacuum cleaners, absorbing all light and matter that pass near them.

A supernova event occurs only once every century or so within our galaxy. Many remnants of supernovas or less dramatic instabilities can be observed

Annie Jump Cannon (1863–1941) examines a star's spectrum.

within our galaxy. One of these, the beautiful Ring Nebula in the constellation Lyra, is easily viewed through a small telescope during the summer months.

Binary Stars

Through your telescope or binoculars, you can see that some stars are actually two stars that travel together (in the same way that the planets move around the Sun). These are called *binary,* or *double, stars.* (Three or more stars that travel together are called *multiple stars.*)

Some binaries are so close that no telescope can separate them. Others have one bright, visible member and one dim, invisible member. If you can see both members of a binary star using a telescope, that binary is classified as a visual binary.

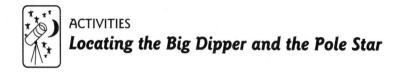

ACTIVITIES
Locating the Big Dipper and the Pole Star

The best times to view the Big Dipper from a mid-northern-latitude observing site are on April and May evenings, when this constellation is high in the sky and about halfway between the northern horizon and the zenith. At this time, the seven major stars of the Big Dipper should be well above the sky glow near the horizon of most populated regions.

If this is your first time viewing the stars from this location, you may want to use a compass to align yourself with the north–south line. Many astronomers use a magnetic compass to find north in an unfamiliar location. Look north as you refer to your chart or star wheel.

Each star chart is accurate only for certain seasons and times. (A star wheel is more versatile than a star chart because you can adjust it for various seasons and times of night.) Hold the chart over your head with ''north'' at the top, and face north. The bright stars visible in the evening sky will correspond to the bright stars on the sky chart.

Once you have found the Big Dipper, look at the two pointer stars. These are the stars in the bowl of the Big Dipper that are farthest from the handle. If you project your line of sight from these two stars to about halfway to the northern horizon, the first fairly bright star that you will see is Polaris, the North Star.

Polaris, which is located within a degree of the north celestial pole, seems to hang suspended in the sky as the other circumpolar stars wheel around it. Polaris is in the tail of Ursa Minor, the Little Bear.

ACTIVITIES
Observing Two Famous Binaries in the Spring Sky

Using the Big Dipper to make your way around the sky, you can find and observe with your telescope two binary stars.

To begin, point your telescope at the second star in the handle of the Big Dipper. Center this star, which goes by the name of Mizar, in the finder scope. Then, focus your low-power eyepiece upon this star. Centered in your eyepiece is perhaps the most famous binary in the sky, Mizar (magnitude 2.4) and Alcor (magnitude 4).

Mizar and Alcor are classified as a visual binary, because you can see each star separately through your telescope (or, in this case, even through binoculars). The members of this pair are about 88 light-years from our solar system. Most observers see Mizar and Alcor as white in color.

At various times in history, a test of clear eyesight was to be able to resolve Mizar and Alcor with the naked eye. But no naked eye, in fact no telescopic image, could have informed us that Mizar and Alcor are both binary stars themselves, so you're actually looking at four stars! The spectroscope, a device that separates light from a star into its component colors, was used to demonstrate the existence of the invisible components of Mizar and Alcor.

To find another binary star, move your eyes from the Mizar/Alcor pair toward the pointer stars on the far side of the Big Dipper's bowl. Keep moving west until you are about halfway between the zenith and the western horizon.

The first magnitude star that you see is Pollux, one of the Gemini Twins. Slightly to the north of Pollux is Castor, a 1.6-magnitude star that is the other Gemini Twin. On a late winter or early spring evening, Gemini will be near the zenith. Now point your telescope toward Castor. A 5-centimeter (2-inch) aperture telescope will be sufficient to separate the main components of Castor. You will observe two blue-white stars.

Both of the visible components of Castor have been revealed to be spectroscopic binaries. In addition, another much fainter spectroscopic binary is also a member of the Castor system. Thus, this naked-eye single star, which appears in your telescope as a beautiful blue-white binary, is actually a stellar sextuple!

Seasonal Stargazing

Whenever the sky is clear, a small telescope or binoculars will reveal many fascinating stars and other distant sky objects. The following activities describe how to find a few of them.

 ACTIVITY
Winter Observations of Orion

One of the most beautiful constellations, Orion the Hunter, can be easily located during the colder months. For a northern latitude observer, this constellation is highest in the sky during late autumn and winter evenings. Orion is about midway between the zenith and the southern horizon at about midnight in December, at around 10 P.M. in January, and at 8 P.M. in February. You should easily find Orion's belt—three stars in a straight line that represents the hunter's waist.

After recognizing Orion's belt, it's easy to find Betelgeuse, a bright, pulsating,

A Brightness Scale for Stars

On a clear night in a rural setting, you can see a few thousand stars with the unassisted eye. The brightest stars you can see have a brightness classified as "visual apparent magnitude 0"; the dimmest stars you can see are classified as "visual apparent magnitude 6." Each time the brightness classifier goes up by one unit of magnitude, the star's brightness decreases by a factor of about 2.5

This means that a 5-magnitude star is 2.5 times as bright as a 6-magnitude star. A 4-magnitude star is 2.5 times as bright as a 5-magnitude star and about 6.25 times as bright as a 6-magnitude star.

Astronomers have developed another magnitude scale to compensate for varying star distances. This is called the absolute magnitude system. Absolute magnitudes are useful in comparing the amount of light emitted by different stars.

Visual apparent magnitudes will be given for some of the stars considered in this chapter, because amateur sky observers tend to concentrate on the brighter objects they can see. Astrophysicists, on the other hand, are more interested in absolute magnitude than in apparent magnitude.

---

giant red star that would easily swallow the Earth if it replaced our Sun. Betelgeuse, which is north of Orion's belt, represents the Hunter's left shoulder (from our point of view). Rigel, a bright blue supergiant, is south of the belt and represents the Hunter's right foot (also from our viewpoint).

When gazing at Orion through a 5-centimeter (2-inch) aperture telescope, you should be able to observe a 7-magnitude attendant to Rigel (the Hunter's right foot). This dimmer companion star is also blue and is visually separated from Rigel by about one-third the diameter of the full Moon. A low-power eyepiece is recommended for viewing both members of the Rigel system at the same time.

After you've become familiar with the stars in Orion, you'll be able to use your telescope or binoculars to see a colorful "star nursery" similar to the one in which the Sun was born almost 5 billion years ago. This object, which is called the Great Nebula in Orion, is southward of Orion's belt and represents his sword.

To find the Great Nebula (also called M42), start at Orion's three belt stars. Move south to about midway between the belt and the level of Rigel and the Hunter's "left foot." The greenish-blue, cloudlike object centered in your telescope's eyepiece is M42.

The Great Nebula in Orion is approximately 1,500 light-years from the Earth and is a few light-years across. In perhaps 100 million years, the infant stars you see in the Great Nebula will have absorbed or blown off most of the dust and gas. Then, this collection of stars will resemble another famous cluster of stars in the winter sky, the Pleiades, also referred to as the Seven Sisters or M45.

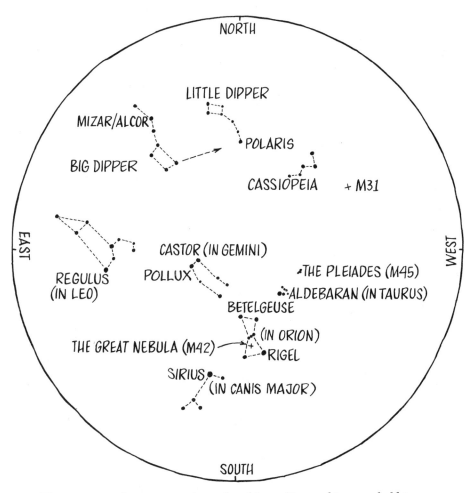

This star map shows some winter sky objects. To use this map, hold it overhead with "North" toward compass direction "North." (This map is made to be accurate especially in February between 8 and 9 P.M., but you can use it any time near then.)

ACTIVITY
Viewing the Pleiades during the Winter

Even though this stellar collection is called the Seven Sisters, the naked-eye observer will usually see only six stars. Through binoculars, many more stars are visible within the Pleiades. A small telescope will reveal a few hundred. This cluster of young stars is about 400 light-years away and has a diameter of perhaps 50 light-years.

To find the Pleiades, first locate Betelgeuse in Orion and Aldebaran in Taurus. Start from Betelgeuse and move along an imaginary line between these two stars. Continue westward past Aldebaran for about the same distance that separates Aldebaran and Betelgeuse. If you focus your telescope on this spot in the sky, you should be able to view the Pleiades.

Even though winter skies are often the clearest, at least from a mid-northern-latitude observing site, temperatures are less than comfortable. If you prefer being outdoors during the warmer nights of spring and summer and don't mind murkier skies, your telescope can be used to find some interesting objects. Don't forget the bug repellent!

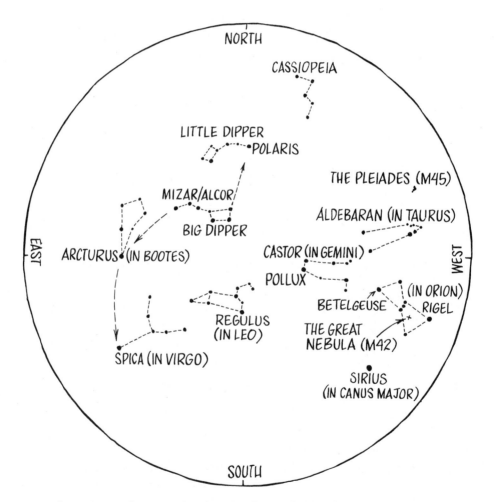

This star map shows some spring sky objects. To use this map, hold it overhead with "North" toward compass direction "North." (This map is made to be accurate especially in April between 8 and 9 P.M., but you can use it any time near then.)

ACTIVITY
Starhopping through the Spring Sky

During the spring, you can practice a technique called starhopping to help you find your way through the sky. By moving your attention among easily located bright stars, you can find much dimmer targets for your telescope, even if you observe through murky urban skies.

Look at the three stars in the handle of the Big Dipper. If you follow the curve or arc of these stars about one-third of the way toward the eastern horizon, you'll come to the bright red star Arcturus, a 0-magnitude star in the constellation Bootes the Herdsman.

Follow the arc still further until you're about one-third of the way between the southeastern horizon and the zenith. The brilliant, blue-white, 1-magnitude star that you see is Spica, in Virgo the Virgin.

On a spring evening, you can use your knowledge of starhopping to locate the star fields of the Milky Way. Go back to the pointer stars of the Big Dipper. Extend the line from these stars through Polaris and almost to the northern horizon. If you point your telescope in this direction, you'll enjoy the spectacle of some of the billions of dim, distant stars of the Milky Way.

You can get another view of this spiral arm of our galaxy by returning to Castor and Pollux in Gemini. You can observe another part of the Milky Way by pointing your telescope about midway between these stars and the western horizon.

ACTIVITY
Summer Observations of an Eclipsing Binary

The summer sky is dominated by the three bright stars that comprise a famous star pattern or asterism called the Summer Triangle. If you're outside at 10 P.M.–midnight in July or 8–10 P.M. in August, the 0-magnitude star Vega will be at or near the zenith (for a mid-northern-latitude observing site). Vega is the brightest star in Lyra the Harp.

About one-third of the way toward the eastern horizon from Vega and within the Milky Way, you come upon the second star in the Summer Triangle, Deneb in Cygnus the Swan. Southeast of Vega and just on the other side of the Milky Way, you will notice brilliant Altair, the third star in the Summer Triangle. Altair is the brightest star in Aquila the Eagle.

Now look about 5 degrees of arc south of Vega. The bright star in your telescope's

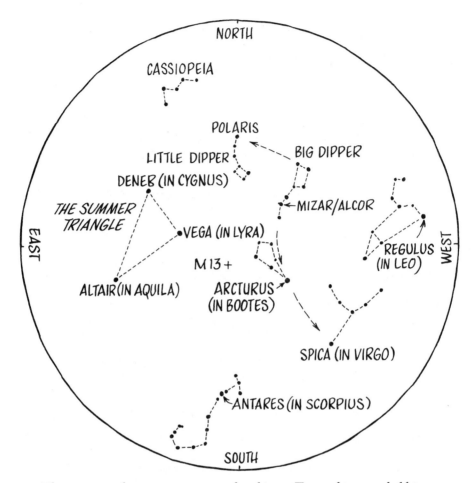

This star map shows some summer sky objects. To use this map, hold it overhead with "North" toward compass direction "North." (This map is made to be accurate especially in July between 9 and 10 P.M., but you can use it any time near then.)

field of view is Beta Lyrae, the second brightest star in Lyra. Use the finder chart for Lyra to help locate this star in the sky.

Beta Lyrae is a fascinating and bizarre star. It's an eclipsing variable, in which a visible star and an invisible star circle a common center of mass. Because of our location in space, sometimes one of the two Beta Lyrae stars passes in front of the other. The visible magnitude of Beta Lyrae changes from 3.4 to 4.3 during a cycle of just under 13 days. Apparently, the brighter Beta Lyrae star (a blue supergiant) is the smallest of the two stars that comprise this binary system. The larger and fainter of the two Beta Lyrae stars has not been observed, even using powerful and sensitive observatory telescopes. Perhaps this huge body is something very exotic such as a black hole! If that were the case, no light could escape from this heavy, small object, and any matter passing near it would be ingested.

About 3 degrees to the east of mysterious Beta Lyrae is Gamma Lyrae, a blue-

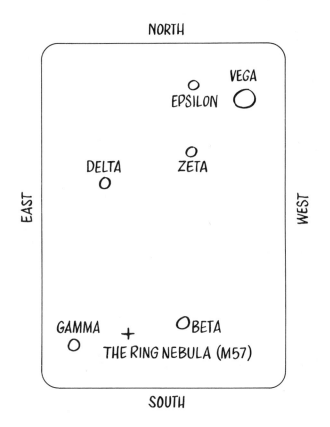

A summer finder chart for stars and the Ring Nebula (M57) in the constellation Lyra

white giant with a visual magnitude of 3.3. Once again, use the finder chart for Lyra to locate this star. You can monitor the brightness variations of Beta Lyrae by comparing variable Beta to constant Gamma. At its brightest, Beta will seem (to your eye) to be about the same brightness as Gamma. Six days later, when Beta is dimmest, it will seem to be about half as bright as Gamma.

Many of the oldest stars in our galaxy are concentrated in *globular clusters.* The separation between neighboring stars in globular clusters is considerably less than the 4.3 light-years that separate the Sun from Alpha/Proxima Centauri, our nearest known stellar neighbors. You can find one of these beautiful star collections in the summer sky and observe it through your telescope.

ACTIVITY
Summer Observations of a Globular Cluster

Return your attention to Vega. If you look to the west of this brillant, blue-white star, the first constellation you encounter is Hercules the Hero. (Hercules is not included on the seasonal star charts in this book because its stars are rather dim.)

On the far end of Hercules from Vega and about 20 degrees to the west of that bright star, a naked-eye observer from a dark observing site will see a "fuzzy ball." At 9 P.M. in July, this object is close to the zenith. Point your telescope, with a low-power eyepiece in place, toward this fuzzy ball in the sky.

Through the eyepiece of a 10-centimeter (4-inch) aperture telescope, you will see literally thousands of stars gathered around a luminous center. This is M13, the most beautiful of the globular clusters. This object, which is a bit smaller in angular size than the full Moon, is approximately 23,000 light-years from the Earth. Most of the hundreds of thousands of stars in M13 are red and billions of years older than our Sun.

As a dying star shrinks toward the white dwarf phase, it may emit puffs of gas that surround it as a transparent shell. Viewed from the Earth, it seems that the star is surrounded by a ring of gas. One of these beautiful objects is easily viewed through your telescope during warm summer nights.

ACTIVITY
Summer Observations of the Ring Nebula

With your telescope, look directly between Beta and Gamma Lyrae. If your telescope has an aperture of at least 7.5 centimeters (3 inches), you'll notice an object like an oval smoke ring in the sky. This is M57, the Ring Nebula in Lyra. Use the finder chart for Lyra to help find M57 in the sky.

The Ring Nebula is a doughnut-shaped gas blob that appears to your telescope's eyepiece to be about the same size as the planet Jupiter. The gas was emitted in the distant past by a hot, blue central star that is not visible in small telescopes. Observers using larger telescopes will notice the blue-green tint of M57.

All of the objects that you've read about so far in this chapter are members of our Milky Way Galaxy. During the autumn, your telescope can be used to view another galaxy. This is M31, the Great Spiral Galaxy in Andromeda. The

The Ring Nebula (Courtesy Palomar Observatory, the California Institute of Technology)

Great Spiral Galaxy is the only extragalactic (outside-of-our-galaxy) object that can be glimpsed from the northern hemisphere with the unassisted eye.

As we explore the vast spaces beyond the Milky Way Galaxy, we encounter a universe consisting of billions of galaxies. Each galaxy, in turn, contains billions of stars. Some galaxies are spirals like the Milky Way and M31. Others are roughly egg-shaped (elliptical) or are classified as irregular. Distances between galaxies are measured in millions or billions of light-years.

ACTIVITY
Autumn Observations of the Great Spiral Galaxy in Andromeda

If you take your telescope outside during a mid-autumn evening at a mid-northern-latitude location, you will notice that the Summer Triangle is far to the west. Orion is rising in the east, and the Pleiades are about halfway between the eastern horizon and the zenith.

The Milky Way is high in the northern sky, and the constellation Andromeda is directly overhead. (Most of the stars in Andromeda are dim, so this constellation is not included on the seasonal star charts.)

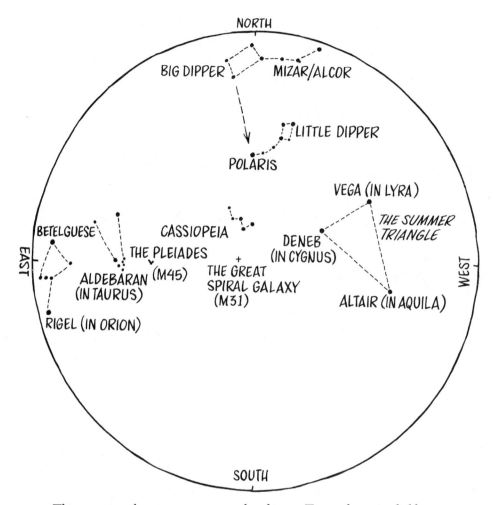

This star map shows some autumn sky objects. To use this map, hold it overhead with "North" toward the compass direction "North." (This map is made to be accurate especially in November between 8 and 9 P.M., but you can use it any time near then.)

Near the zenith, you will notice an irregular cloudlike object that is a bit larger than 2 degrees of arc (the visual width of four full Moons) across, at its greatest extent. This is the Great Spiral Galaxy in Andromeda, which is also known as M31.

Unfortunately, you won't be able to see through the telescope the magnificent spiral structure of this galaxy that can be seen in photographs. Through your low-power eyepiece, none of the 100 billion or so stars that constitute this near twin of our galaxy will be resolved. That's not surprising, because M31 is 2 million or so light-years away from our solar system. Even through a small telescope, though, you'll be able to see some hint of M31's spiral structure—a long, oval patch that brightens toward the center.

Under higher magnification, the observer may be fortunate enough to spot a circular blob of light about 25 arc-minutes (a bit less than one lunar diameter) to the south of M31's center. This dwarf elliptical galaxy (called M32) is a satellite to the Great Spiral Galaxy and is not visible to the naked eye.

Southern Skies

If you travel to a Southern Hemisphere location, you will be able to observe many sky objects that are below the horizon at a Northern Hemisphere site. One of these is Alpha Centauri, the 0-magnitude star that is our Sun's closest interstellar neighbor.

Below the equator, you'll also be able to observe the Clouds of Magellan. These irregular galaxies are considerably closer to us than M31 in Andromeda, but they are much smaller.

Planning a Star Watch

After you learn a bit about the stars, you'll want to begin planning your first stellar observing session. Together with your telescope, it's a good idea to bring a star wheel or finder chart, so that you'll be able to find your way around the heavens. A star atlas will also help make your stellar observing sessions more productive.

Before your observing session, try to select a few targets from the millions of stars visible through your telescope. Use your star atlas, star wheel, or finder chart to pick the best stars, star clouds, or gas clouds in the sky on a particular night. Some advance planning will make your star-viewing session infinitely more rewarding.

Also, you should remember that your eyes will become dark-adapted after a few minutes at the telescope. To maintain your eyes' dark adaptation, you should use a red-tinted flashlight when you refer to your star wheel, star atlas, or finder chart.

★ 7 ★
Observing the Sun

uring the daytime, your telescope need not sit idle. Even on the sunniest day, you can still observe the nearest star—our Sun! However, its very important for the solar observer to always remember the following caution: **NEVER, NEVER look directly at the Sun with either the unassisted eye or your telescope unless you have the proper neutral density filters.** In this chapter, you'll learn about some safe ways to look at the Sun.

Physical Properties of Our Sun

Using your imaginary scale from Chapter 5, you would learn that the Sun dwarfs the various planets in the solar system. The Sun would weigh in at about 1,000 Jupiter-weights and 300,000 Earth-weights. The physical radius of this yellow, hydrogen-burning star is about 700,000 kilometers (400,000 miles). A million Earths would easily fit within the Sun.

Like other stars, the Sun shines by thermonuclear fusion. Deep within this star's interior, matter is constantly being converted into energy. Even though the Sun has radiated enough energy to heat more than a billion Earths for the past few billion years, the fuel reserves within the Sun are ample for at least another 5 billion years.

The visible surface of the Sun is called the *photosphere* and has a temperature of 10,000°F (6000°C). This is considerably cooler than the million-degree interior! You can safely view features of the solar photosphere using a homebuilt projection screen or a strong neutral density (ND) filter attached to your telescope's aperture.

Through a properly protected telescope with an aperture of 7.5–10 centimeters (3–4 inches), you'll be able to view temporary disturbances on the photosphere called *sunspots.* The sunspots appear darker than the surrounding photosphere because they are a bit cooler, but still a very respectable 7000–8000°F (4000° or 4500°C)!

The Sun has two atmospheric layers—the chromosphere and corona. These layers can only be viewed using some rather expensive accessories or during a solar eclipse.

Astronomers study features on the photosphere and other solar layers in order to monitor solar activity. By observing sunspots, you can keep track of the solar activity cycle. When the Sun is very active, many sunspots are visible on the photosphere, and solar emissions (the solar wind) can interfere with shortwave radio reception. The solar activity cycle has a time period of 22 years.

Safely Observing the Daytime Star

When observing the Sun, it is a good idea to remember the sad experience of Galileo, the first telescopic astronomer. As the discoverer of sunspots, Galileo paid for his many hours of viewing the Sun through his unfiltered telescope with permanent eye damage.

There is no reason for a modern astronomer to repeat Galileo's mistake. To view sunspots safely, you can purchase (for about $50) or easily construct a projection screen that can be attached to your telescope's eyepiece. If you have a bit more money (less than $160), you can purchase a very efficient and safe solar neutral density filter for any telescope with an aperture of 20 centimeters (8 inches) or less.

You should always make sure that your finder scope is covered during solar observing sessions so that you do not accidentally glance through it at the magnified image of the Sun. Also, don't be tempted by less expensive (but less effective) filters that fit over the telescope eyepiece instead of the aperture. If you purchase a solar aperture filter, protect both your eyes and your telescope by always making sure that it is securely in place before you view the Sun. **The first, second, and third rules of solar observing are to NEVER, NEVER, NEVER even think of glancing at the Sun except through a properly outfitted telescope.**

 ACTIVITY
Constructing a Solar Projection Screen for Your Telescope

The accompanying drawing shows a solar projection screen that you can construct for your telescope. Use four plywood struts as the supporting structure and fasten a piece of tracing paper to the struts as shown, using masking tape or glue. This is the projection screen.

You'll want to attach the struts to your eyepiece. This can be done with wire, rubber bands, or a gripping material such as Velcro.® The trick is to arrange your projection screen on the eyepiece so that it doesn't fall off. You may also want to use black cloth wrapped around the screen-supporting structure so that the only sunlight striking the projection screen is light that has been transmitted through your telescope. This will increase the contrast of the solar disk image on the projection screen.

Now, with your projection screen or ND aperture filter in place and your finder scope covered, you're ready to observe. You might be wondering how to direct your telescope toward the Sun with the finder scope inoperative. What you do is concentrate upon the telescope's shadow as you point it toward the Sun. When the shadow seems smallest—essentially circular—the Sun is centered within the telescope's field of view. Now it is quite safe to view the solar

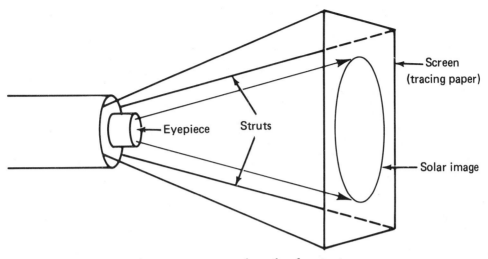

A projection screen for safe solar viewing

disk through the telescope's low- or medium-power eyepiece (with filter or projection screen in place, of course).

Sunspots

If the sky is reasonably clear, you should be able to distinguish some sunspots as areas that are a bit darker than the surrounding photosphere. At first, you may think that these dark spots on the Sun's face are just smudges on your eyepiece, ND aperture filter, or projection screen. Try nudging the telescope tube gently with your finger. If the dark spots jiggle with the Sun's disk, they are indeed sunspots!

You'll notice that some of these stand alone; others are gathered in groups. The number of sunspots and sunspot groups is a measure of solar activity.

ACTIVITIES
Viewing Sunspots

With a telescope aperture of 7.5–10 centimeters (3–4 inches), a projection screen or neutral density (ND) aperture filter, and a magnification of no more than 70X–100X, observing sunspots can be a safe and very rewarding experience.

As an initial sunspot-viewing activity, you may want to observe the structure of a typical sunspot. You'll notice that the dark central region, or *umbra* is surrounded by a less dark region called the *penumbra*.

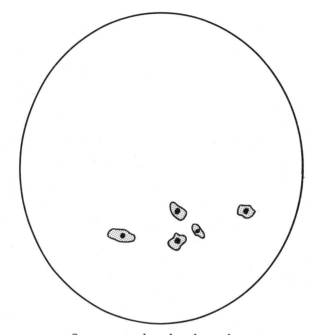

Sunspots on the solar photosphere

The Sun rotates once every 25 days. Since sunspots and groups of sunspots have a lifetime measured in weeks, one method of gauging solar rotation is to make regular sketches of the solar photosphere at intervals of a few days. A recognizable sunspot group will take about 12 days to completely cross the visible face of the Sun.

If you make regular sketches of the Sun's appearance, you can actually monitor changes to a sunspot or sunspot group during its lifetime. With a reticle eyepiece, you can compare the angular size of a sunspot to that of the Sun. The Sun, which has an angular size of about ½ degree of arc, has a diameter of 1,400,000 kilometers (800,000 miles). Even the smallest sunspot you view could probably swallow the Earth in a single gulp!

By counting sunspots and sunspot groups, you can estimate solar activity—the more visible the sunspots and groups of sunspots, the more active the Sun. Some solar observers regularly report their sunspot counts to the solar group of the American Association of Variable Star Observers (AAVSO), which is located in Cambridge, Massachusetts.

The level of sunspot activity is very important to people living on the Earth and to astronauts in orbit. A large number of sunspots indicate an active Sun. Accordingly, the amount of radioactive particles from the Sun reaching the Earth (the solar wind) increases. Shortwave radio communication may also be disrupted, and astronauts may be required to return to Earth. Some airplanes fly at lower altitudes when the Sun is very active, to protect the passengers and crew from exposure to particles emitted by the active Sun.

Solar Eclipses

No astronomer can resist the opportunity of turning his or her instrument sky-ward when the Sun, Earth, and Moon occasionally line up with the Moon between the Sun and the Earth, bringing about a solar eclipse (see diagram). Predictions of eclipses are included in many astronomical publications, includ-ing monthly magazines, almanacs, and handbooks. This information will allow you the opportunity to prepare if an eclipse visible in your area will occur in the near future. Some dedicated amateurs travel thousands of miles to enjoy the few moments of a distant total solar eclipse.

 ACTIVITY
Observing a Solar Eclipse

During a total solar eclipse, the Sun's visible surface (the photosphere) is entirely covered by the Moon's disk. The Sun's inner atmospheric layer, or chromosphere, may then be visible as a bright ring around the Moon's disk.

As the dark Moon covers the blindingly bright photosphere, the Sun's outer at-mospheric layer, or corona, becomes visible. As skies darken, the stars become visible in the daytime sky. Sometimes during a total solar eclipse, prominences are visible extending above the obscured Sun. These are brilliant bridges of light in the chromo-sphere, which reveal a solar flare in progress. Brilliant lights may dance through the sky as beams of sunlight pass between mountains near the Moon's edge.

The corona of the Sun is never the same from one eclipse to the next. Sometimes,

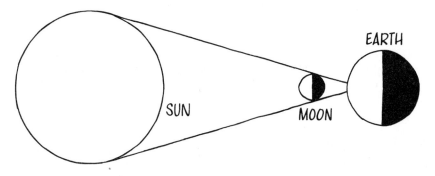

During a solar eclipse, the Moon is between the Earth and the Sun. (Note: Distances and sizes are not to scale.)

it seems like a bright, symmetrical ring surrounding the eclipsed photosphere. At other times, bright streamers extend out from the corona for many solar diameters. Try to sketch your impression of the solar corona during the few minutes that the Sun is eclipsed.

———————————

APPENDIX A
Astrovendors

The following is a partial list of some major U.S. vendors of astronomical equipment. Catalogs ordered from some of these companies can be used in conjunction with Chapter 3 to help you in selecting astronomical equipment. In addition, many smaller astronomical equipment vendors advertise regularly in the pages of *Astronomy* and *Sky & Telescope*. Other sources of astronomical equipment are department, electronic, and toy stores and hobby shops.

Vendor Name	Vendor Address (and Toll-free Phone Number)
Adorama	42 W. 18th St., New York, NY 10011 (800) 223–2500
Cosmos Ltd.	9215 Waukegan Rd., Morton Grove, IL 60053
Edmund Scientific Co.	101 E. Gloucester Pike, Barrington, NJ 08007
Focus Camera Inc.	4419–21 13th Ave., Brooklyn, NY 11219 (800) 221–0828
Lumicon	2111 Research Drive #5S, Livermore, CA 94550 (800) 767–9576
Meade Instruments Co.	1675 Toronto Way, Costa Mesa, CA 92626
Orion Telescope Center	2450 17th Ave., P.O. Box 1158, Santa Cruz, CA 95061 (800) 447–1001. In California, (800) 443–1001
Roger W. Tuthill, Inc.	Box 1086ST, Mountainside, NJ 07902 (800) 223–1063
University Optics Inc.	P. O. Box 1205, Ann Arbor, MI 48106 (800) 521–2828
Wholesale Optics	29 Kingswood Road, Danbury, CT 06811

APPENDIX B
A Note about Measurement

When discussing the distance between celestial objects or the physical sizes of these sky objects, most astronomers use metric measurements rather than the English measurements of inches, feet, and miles. It's easy to convert between the different measurement systems. The following table lists some common conversions:

1 kilometer	= 1,000	meters
1 meter	= 100	centimeters
1 meter	= 1,000,000	microns
1 centimeter	= 10	millimeters
1 inch	= 2.54	centimeters
1 foot	= 0.305	meter
1 mile	= 1.609	kilometers

When astronomers talk about distances of millions or billions of kilometers, they usually use the astronomical unit (abbreviated AU) and the light-year. The average distance between the Earth and the Sun is 1 AU. One light-year is the distance that light, moving at 300,000 kilometers (186,000 miles) per second, moves in one year. These units can be converted to more familiar units, for example:

1 astronomical unit = 150 million kilometers = 93 million miles
1 light-year = 63,290 astronomical units

The metric system uses *mass* in calculating the weight of an object. Mass is a measure of the amount of material within an object, or the resistance of that body to changes in its motion. The basic units of mass are the gram and kilogram. In the United States, however, the weight in pounds of an object at the surface of the Earth is used for nonscientific applications. The weight (in pounds) is a measure of the gravitational attraction that the Earth exerts upon an object near its surface. Conversions between mass and Earth-weight are:

1 pound = 454 grams
1 kilogram = 2.205 pounds

APPENDIX C
Reading List: To Dig Deeper

If you are interested in learning more about some of the topics considered in this book, you might want to investigate some of the following references. Remember that good sources of astronomical information are the monthly magazines *Odyssey* (which is targeted at young amateur astronomers), *Astronomy*, and *Sky & Telescope*.

Specially for Young Astronomers

Branley, F. *Uranus: The Seventh Planet*. New York: Crowell/Harper & Row, 1988.

Chaple, G. F., Jr. *Exploring with a Telescope*. New York: Franklin Watts, 1988.

Cole, J. *The Magic School Bus Lost the Solar System*. New York: Scholastic, 1990.

Gardner, R. *Projects in Space Science*. New York: Simon & Schuster, Messner, 1988.

Jobb, J. *The Night Sky Book*. Boston: Little, Brown & Co., 1977.

Krupp, E. C. *The Big Dipper and You*. New York: William Morrow & Co., 1989.

Lauber, P. *Journey to the Planets*. New York: Crown, 1987.

Mammana, D. *The Night Sky*. Philadelphia: Running Press, 1989.

Moche, D. *Astronomy Today*. New York: Random House, 1986.

Ride, S., and O. Okie. *To Space and Back*. New York: Lothrup, Lee & Shepard, 1986.

Some Handbooks, Guidebooks, and Atlases

Baker, D. *The Henry Holt Guide to Astronomy*. New York: Henry Holt, 1990.

Burnham, R., Jr. *Burnham's Celestial Handbook: An Observer's Guide to the Universe Beyond the Solar System*. New York: Dover, 1978.

Matloff, G. L. *The Urban Astronomer*. New York: John Wiley & Sons, 1991.

Menzel, D. H., and J. M. Pasachoff. *A Field Guide to Stars and Planets*. Boston: Houghton Mifflin, 1983.

Raymo, C. *365 Starry Nights*. Englewood Cliffs, NJ: Prentice Hall, 1982.

Ridpath, I. *Norton's 2000.0 Star Atlas and Reference Handbook*. Belmont, MA: Sky Publishing, 1990.

Sanford, J. *Observing the Constellations*. New York: Simon & Schuster, 1989.

Sherrod, P. C., and T. L. Koed. *A Complete Manual for Amateur Astronomy*. Englewood Cliffs, NJ: Prentice Hall, 1981.

Annuals

The Air Almanac. U.S. Naval Observatory, Washington, DC, and Her Majesty's Stationary Office, London, UK.

Astronomical Calendar. Astronomical Workshop, Furman University, Greenville, SC 29613.

The Observer's Handbook. The Royal Astronomical Society of Canada, Toronto, Canada.

Glossary of Astronomical Terms

Aberration, Optical: A problem in a telescope in which different light rays are brought to focus in different locations.

Absolute Magnitude: A measure of star brightness that compensates for the distances to different stars. (Compare apparent magnitude.)

Absorption: A process by which matter can remove photons from a light beam. The photon energy energizes, or excites, the absorbing atoms.

Alt–az Mount: A telescope mount that allows the user to easily locate celestial objects. Alt–az stands for "altitude–azimuth."

Aperture: The size of a telescope's main lens or mirror.

Apparent Magnitude: A measure of star brightness based on the stars that can be seen with the unassisted eye. (Compare absolute magnitude.)

Asterism: A convenient and obvious star pattern in the sky.

Asteroid: A minor planet. Most asteroids circle the Sun between the orbits of Mars and Jupiter, the so-called "asteroid belt."

Astronomical Unit: The average Earth–Sun separation, about 93 million miles (150 million kilometers). The astronomical unit is often abbreviated as AU.

Astrophysics: The branch of physics that deals with astronomical objects.

Binary (or Double) Star: A pair of stars that are relatively close to each other in space and revolve around a common center of gravity.

Binoculars: A refractive telescope that can be used with both eyes. Unlike most astronomical telescopes, the image through binoculars is right side up.

Black Hole: The final evolutionary state of a star originally much larger than our Sun. The star's matter has become so compressed that even light cannot escape being sucked into a black hole.

Boresight: To align a telescope and its finder scope.

Catadioptic Telescope: A telescope that combines aspects of a reflector and a refractor.

Circumpolar Constellation: A constellation that is visible at all times of the year from the Northern Hemisphere.

Clock Drive: An electrical device that allows a telescope to follow a celestial object across the sky by automatically correcting for the Earth's rotation.

Color Filter: An optical component that allows only certain colors through to the observer.

Comet: A solar system body consisting of layers of rock as well as methane, ammonia, and water ice.

Constellation: A convenient pattern of stars in the sky. These are often named for ancient heroes, animals, and familiar objects.

Conjunction: A close alignment of two or more celestial bodies.

Declination: The celestial equivalent of latitude.

Eclipse: An astronomical event that occurs when one celestial body passes behind another, from the point of view of an observer on the Earth. (See lunar eclipse and solar eclipse.)

Ecliptic: The apparent path of the Sun and the planets across the sky.

Electromagnetic Radiation/Spectrum: Those forms of radiation (gamma rays, X rays, ultraviolet light, visible light, infrared light, and radio waves) that move through space at the speed of light (300,000 kilometers or 186,000 miles per second). Electromagnetic radiation has both wavelike and particlelike characteristics.

Ellipse: The approximately egg-shaped orbit of a planet around the Sun.

Equatorial Mount: A telescope mount that allows the observer to track celestial objects as the Earth's rotation causes them to move across the sky.

Eyepiece: The lens or group of lenses on a telescope that directs light to the observer's eye.

Finder Scope: A small telescope that is boresighted with a larger instrument so that both point in the same direction. The finder scope is used to locate and center the image of a celestial object in the larger instrument's field of view.

Field of View (FOV): The angular extent of the sky that can be viewed at any one time through a telescope.

Focal Length: The distance between a lens (or mirror) and where light rays from a distant source passing through that optical component converge.

Focal Plane: The plane where light passing through a lens (or mirror) from a distant source converges.

Frequency: The number of waves (of light, sound, etc.) that reach an observer per second.

Galaxy: A vast "star city" containing billions of stars. Galaxies can be either spiral, elliptical, or irregular in shape.

Gamma Ray: The highest energy form of electromagnetic radiation.

Gas Giant Planet: A world, such as Jupiter, Saturn, Uranus, and Neptune, that is much larger than the Earth, has a thick atmosphere, many satellites, and a system of rings. Gas Giants are also called *Jovian planets*.

Geocentric World View: An obsolete theory of the solar system that placed a stationary Earth at the center of the universe. The Moon, Sun, and planets circled the Earth.

Globular Cluster: A collection of hundreds of thousands or millions of usually older stars in a comparatively small volume of space.

Gravity: The force of attraction between different material objects in the universe.

Greenhouse Effect: The heating of a planetary surface when gases in that planet's lower atmosphere absorb and trap infrared radiation.

Heliocentric World View: The correct theory of the solar system in which the Earth and planets circle the Sun and the Moon circles the Earth.

Inferior Planet: A planet closer to the Sun than the Earth is: Mercury and Venus.

Infrared Radiation: Electromagnetic radiation less energetic than visible light.

Ionosphere: An upper region of the Earth's atmosphere in which high-energy forms of electromagnetic radiation (gamma rays and X rays) are absorbed.

Jovian Planet: See gas giant planet.

Latitudinal Markings: Structures on a planet's visible surface that are parallel to that planet's equator.

Lens: An optical component that alters the path of a light ray by refraction. Most lenses are constructed of glass.

Light-gathering Power: The property of a telescope that makes an object that is dim or invisible to the unassisted eye seem brighter.

Light-year: The distance that electromagnetic radiation travels in one year (about 63,000 astronomical units). The light-year is the basic measure of distances beyond our solar system.

Lunar Eclipse: An event that occurs when the Earth lines up directly between the Moon and the Sun.

Magnification: Making a small object seem larger.

Main Sequence Star: A stable star, such as our Sun, in which hydrogen is converted into helium and energy.

Mare (Maria, *pl.*): A flat, dark area of the Moon's surface that was thought by early telescopic astronomers to be a sea.

Mass: A measure of the amount of material in a physical object, or the resistance of that object to changes in its motion.

Meteor: A "shooting star." A small piece of dust or ice (usually from the tail of a passing comet) that burns up as it passes through the Earth's atmosphere.

Meteorite: A chunk of rock from space, usually from an asteroid, that survives passage through the Earth's atmosphere to reach the surface of our planet.

Mirror: An optical component that alters the path of a light ray by reflection.

Multiple Star: A gravitational arrangement of more than two stars.

Nadir: The point in the sky directly below your feet and on the other side of the Earth.

Naked-eye Planet: The planets Mercury, Venus, Mars, Jupiter, and Saturn, which can be seen without the aid of binoculars or a telescope.

Nebula: An interstellar cloud of dust, gas, and often stars.

Neutral Density (ND) Filter: A device that equally reduces the intensity of all colors of light transmitted to the observer.

Neutron Star: The final evolutionary state of a star that was originally somewhat larger than our Sun. Neutron stars are very compact with all the matter of the star in a volume about equal to that of our Moon.

Objective Lens: The main lens of a refracting telescope.

Orbit: The closed path of one celestial object revolving about another.

Ozone: A form of oxygen that is usually found in the Earth's stratosphere and that is an efficient absorber of ultraviolet radiation from the Sun.

Penumbra: The less dark outer region of a sunspot.

Perigee: The closest approach of the Moon or an artificial satellite orbiting the Earth to our planet.

Period: The time between alternate peaks of a wave.

Photon: The smallest unit of electromagnetic radiation.

Photosphere: The visible surface of the Sun.

Planet: A celestial object that revolves around a star and shines by reflected light.

Pressure: A measure of force (weight) per unit area.

Primary Mirror: The largest mirror of a reflecting telescope.

Proper Motion: A long-term shift in stars' positions in the sky caused by the fact that they are all revolving (as is our Sun) around the center of the Milky Way Galaxy.

Protosun: An infant star enshrouded in gas and dust.

Pulsars: Neutron stars that emit pulsating radio signals.

Pupil: The variable-width opening that admits light to the eye.

Reflection: Altering the path of a light ray by bouncing it off a surface, such as a mirror.

Reflector: A telescope using mirrors as the major optical components.

Refraction: Altering the path of a light ray by passing it from one transparent medium to another (air to glass or air to water.)

Refractor: A telescope using lenses as the major optical components.

Resolution: The property of a telescope that allows an observer to view fine details on a distant object.

Reticle Eyepiece: A telescope eyepiece equipped with an illuminated internal scale that allows you to measure the size of a celestial object or to determine angular distances between objects.

Revolution: The motion of one celestial object about another.

Right Ascension: The celestial equivalent of longitude.

Rotation: The spin of an object about its north–south axis.

Satellite: A natural or artificial celestial object that revolves around a planet and shines by reflected light.

Scattering: A phenomenon in which photons of electromagnetic radiation bounce off particles of matter.

Secondary Mirror: The smaller mirror of a reflecting telescope.

Setting Circles: An accessory used with an equatorial mount that helps the astronomer locate dim celestial objects.

Solar Eclipse: An event that occurs when the Moon passes directly between the Sun and Earth.

Solar Wind: A high-velocity stream of electrically charged particles emitted by the Sun.

Star: A celestial object that generates the light by which it shines.

Star Finder: A tool used in locating celestial objects, such as a star atlas, star chart, or star wheel.

Stratosphere: A mid-layer of the Earth's atmosphere in which ozone absorbs much of the ultraviolet radiation reaching the Earth from the Sun.

Sunspots: Relatively cool and dark regions on the photosphere.

Superior Planet: A planet farther from the Sun than the Earth is: Mars, Jupiter, Saturn, Uranus, Neptune, and Pluto.

Supernova: The explosive death of a star originally much larger than our Sun. (A less dramatic stellar eruption is called a *nova.*)

Telescopic Planets: Those planets of the solar system (Uranus, Neptune, and Pluto) that cannot be observed with the unaided eye.

Terminator: The dividing line between dark and light portions of the Moon or any other celestial body.

Terraforming: A possible far-future process whereby conditions on a planet like Mars could be altered to more closely resemble those on the Earth.

Terrestrial Planet: The planets Mercury, Venus, Earth, and Mars. They are relatively small, have comparatively thin atmospheres, and few or no natural satellites.

Thermal Equilibrium: The condition existing when your telescope is at the same temperature as the surrounding atmosphere.

Thermonuclear Reaction: The basic energy source of the universe. Deep in the interior of the Sun and other stars, hydrogen atoms are combined to form helium atoms and electromagnetic energy.

Transit: An astronomical event that occurs when a celestial object is observed to pass in front of a larger sky object.

Troposphere: The lowest layer of the Earth's atmosphere in which carbon dioxide and water vapor absorb infrared radiation.

Ultraviolet Light: A form of electromagnetic radiation that is more energetic than visible light but less energetic than X rays or gamma rays.

Umbra: The dark central region of a sunspot.

Variable Star: A star with varying brightness. Some brightness variations are caused by internal pulsations. Others are caused when one member of a binary pair passes in front of, or eclipses, the other.

Wavelength: The distance between the peaks of two alternate waves.

Wave Velocity: The rate at which a wave moves through a medium.

White Dwarf: The final state of a Sunlike star, in which thermonuclear reactions have ceased and the star has collapsed to a physical size smaller than that of the Earth.

Zenith: The point in the sky directly above an observer's head.

Zodiac: A group of 12 constellations near the ecliptic.

Index